R. W. Hanbury

Celtic Ornaments found in Ireland

R. W. Hanbury

Celtic Ornaments found in Ireland

ISBN/EAN: 9783741197277

Manufactured in Europe, USA, Canada, Australia, Japa

Cover: Foto ©Thomas Meinert / pixelio.de

Manufactured and distributed by brebook publishing software
(www.brebook.com)

R. W. Hanbury

Celtic Ornaments found in Ireland

Ordered, by The House of Commons, to be Printed,
1 May 1899.

LONDON:
PRINTED FOR HER MAJESTY'S STATIONERY OFFICE,
BY WYMAN AND SONS, LIMITED, FETTER LANE, E.C.

And to be purchased, either directly or through any Bookseller, from
EYRE AND SPOTTISWOODE, EAST HARDING STREET, FLEET STREET, E.C., and
32, ABINGDON STREET, WESTMINSTER, S.W., or
JOHN MENZIES & CO., 12, HANOVER STREET, EDINBURGH, and
90, WEST NILE STREET, GLASGOW; or
HODGES, FIGGIS & CO., LIMITED, 104, GRAFTON STREET, DUBLIN.

1899.

COPY of Report of a Committee appointed by the Lords Commissioners of Her Majesty's Treasury to inquire into the circumstances under which certain Celtic Ornaments found in Ireland were recently offered for Sale to the British Museum, and to consider the relations between the British Museum and the Museums of Edinburgh and Dublin with regard to the acquisition and retention of objects of Antiquarian and Historic interest; with Evidence, Appendices, and Index.

TREASURY MINUTE APPOINTING THE COMMITTEE.

Treasury Chambers, Whitehall,
24th October 1898.

The First Lord calls the attention of the Board to sundry proceedings in Parliament connected with certain antiquities discovered in Ireland and purchased by the Trustees of the British Museum.

It is unnecessary for Mr. Balfour to refer in detail to these proceedings; but his answer to a question put to him in the House of Commons on the 21st July records a pledge of inquiry into the relations between the British Museum and those of Edinburgh and Dublin, and he is now in a position to recommend the appointment of a Committee composed of the following gentlemen:—

Right Hon. Lord Rathmore (chairman).
Right Hon. John Morley, M.P.
Right Hon. Sir John Lubbock, Bart., M.P.
Sir John Evans, K.C.B.
Right Hon. Sir Herbert Maxwell, Bart., M.P.
Sir Thomas Esmonde, Bart., M.P.

Mr. Balfour suggests that the terms of reference to such Committee should be as follows:—

To inquire into the circumstances under which certain Celtic ornaments found in Ireland were recently offered for sale to the British Museum.

To consider and suggest regulations for avoiding undue competition between museums supported out of public funds in Scotland and Ireland on the one hand, and the British Museum on the other, for the acquisition of objects of antiquarian or historic interest; and for ensuring that in the case of objects which from their origin or associations are of peculiar interest either to Scotland or Ireland, the museum situated in the country so interested should be afforded an opportunity of purchasing them before they are acquired by any other institutions supported out of public funds: and

To consider whether any, and if so what, relaxations should be made in the regulations (statutory or otherwise) which prevent the British Museum parting with objects which it has once acquired.

My Lords concur, and are pleased to appoint Mr. E. G. Harman, of their department, to be secretary to the Committee.

Confidential.]

REPORT.

MAY IT PLEASE YOUR LORDSHIPS,

We have considered the several questions referred to us by your Lordships' Minute of the 24th October, and we have the honour to report upon them to your Lordships as follows:—

I.—"To inquire into the circumstances under which certain Celtic ornaments found in Ireland were recently offered for sale to the British Museum." Reference.

The objects mentioned in the first paragraph of your Lordships' Reference Evidence,
consist of: 4.

1. A hollow collar, in two sections, with elaborate repoussé ornament of eccentric curves.

2. A model boat with eight thwarts (originally nine), and a number of oars, spars, &c.

3. A hemispherical bowl of thin metal, with four rings at the edges for suspension.

4. A solid gold torc of stout wire, with a thinner wire twisted round it.

5. One half of a similar torc.

6. A necklace, formed of three plaited chains, with a peculiar fastening, and

7. A thin, single chain necklace of the same plaiting.

These objects are stated to have been found early in 1896 by a farm labourer 3.
whilst ploughing the lands of Mr. Joseph Gibson, in the neighbourhood of Limavady, in the North West of Ireland; and they afterwards came—how it does not clearly appear—into the possession of Mr. Gribben, a jeweller, of Belfast, from whom they were purchased by Mr. Day, who is a collector of antiquities, a Member of the Royal Irish Academy, and a Fellow of the Society of Antiquaries of London.

The above statement as to the circumstances under which these articles were discovered was furnished to us by Sir Patrick Coll, Chief Crown Solicitor for Ireland,
as the result of inquiries made by the police upon the spot (but at a subsequent See Appen-
period); and he added that the facts so stated led him to the conclusion that the dix I.
articles were Treasure Trove, and that they could now be proved to be so if the persons who knew the facts would give truthful evidence. The Attorney General for
Ireland, in answer to a question put to him in the House of Commons, during the March 20,
last Session of Parliament, expressed his opinion to the same effect. 1896,
715.

The law and practice as to Treasure Trove in Ireland, so far as it is necessary for our purpose to consider it, may be shortly stated as follows:—

"Treasure Trove," says Sir Edward Coke, "is when any gold or silver in coin plate or bullion hath been of ancient time hidden, wheresoever it be found, whereof no person can prove any property," and such treasure belongs to the Sovereign by Prerogative (unless an express grant of the franchise of Treasure Trove can be established). It is usually given up to the Police, or reported to the Government, and
concealment of it is an indictable offence punishable by fine and imprisonment. 131.
The disposal of Treasure Trove is in the absolute discretion of the Treasury, acting Cf. 5 [illegible]
on behalf of the Crown, but for many years the Treasury has had no direct dealings Act 1 Vic.
with Treasure Trove in Ireland, the whole responsibility in connection therewith Cap. 2,
having been delegated to the Royal Irish Academy. One hundred pounds Sec. 2.
(included in the Royal Irish Academy Grant-in-Aid) is annually provided by 272 283
Parliament for rewards to discoverers of Treasure Trove, and this sum can be accumulated from year to year. The Academy posts notices in the Constabulary
barracks and other places throughout Ireland informing the public that payments 266, 378.
for such articles, higher than those which could be obtained from dealers, will be awarded to finders of them who deliver them up to the Police. The Government always give the Royal Irish Academy the refusal of Treasure Trove thus recovered in Ireland.

If therefore the hoard found near Limavady be Treasure Trove it ought according
to law to have been delivered up to the Police or the Government of Ireland, and it
would in that case no doubt have been handed over to the Academy to be kept
under their charge in the National Museum of Ireland. That Museum contains one
107, 711 of the most valuable series of this kind of gold ornaments now existing, though,
775 according to the evidence of Mr. Read, the best collection of general objects belonging
to the class of late Celtic antiquities is to be found in the British Museum.

It appears, however, that Mr. Day having obtained possession of these objects
in the manner above described offered them for sale to the British Museum under
the circumstances which are set forth in the following memorandum prepared for
8 us by Sir Edward Maunde Thompson:—

"In the autumn of 1896, Mr. Robert Day, F.S.A., a well-known collector of works of art and antiquities, living in Cork, informed Mr. C. H. Read, the Keeper of the British and Mediæval Antiquities in the British Museum, that he had secured from a silversmith some very fine gold ornaments of Late Celtic work. Mr. Read, who is also the Secretary of the Society of Antiquaries of London, suggested to Mr. Day that the Society should have an opportunity of seeing them.

"Accordingly Mr. Day exhibited the ornaments at a meeting of the Society on the 14th January, 1897; and an account of the meeting appeared in the 'Athenæum' newspaper of the 30th January.

"Meanwhile Mr. Read having expressed an opinion to Mr. Day that these important objects should pass to the British Museum, should he at any time part with them, negotiations followed, with the result that Mr. Day offered the collection to the Trustees of the British Museum for the sum of 600*l*.

"Mr. Read recommended the purchase to the Trustees in a report of the 8th of April, 1897.

"The Trustees sanctioned the purchase at a meeting of the Standing Committee on the 9th of April, 1897. The order for payment was issued on the 12th of May.

"E. MAUNDE THOMPSON."

At the meeting of the Society of Antiquaries above mentioned, a paper was read
by Mr. A. J. Evans, Keeper of the Ashmolean Museum, Oxford, in which he said:
534 "There is at least no question as to the indigenous Celtic character of the most
important relic contained in the Irish hoard. The hollow gold collar, with its bold
repoussé designs, is undoubtedly an ancient Irish fabric, and is at the same time the
finest example existing of this class of work." Mr. Evans seems also to have been of
opinion that probably the golden boat, and possibly the other objects, with the
exception of the triple chain, were of Irish origin. On the other hand, Mr. C. H.
139 Read contended, in the course of his evidence before us, that there was no proof that
any one of these articles was made in Ireland.

243 Dr. Atkinson, who is Secretary to the Council of the Royal Irish Academy,
stated to us that that body had no knowledge of the "find" in question until the
publication of the "Athenæum" newspaper (January 30th, 1897), that they then
immediately appointed a Committee to consider the circumstances thus disclosed to
them, and that he was directed to make enquiries of Sir Patrick Coll (as Chief Crown
Solicitor for Ireland), by whom he was told that the Irish Government had no
information on the subject and that they could not move the Constabulary to act
until further particulars were furnished as to the time and place of the discovery.
No other steps were taken by the Academy from that time (February 1897)
until February 1898, and it appears to us that if this treasure had been upon the
market throughout that interval there would have been some danger of its being
sold out of the country and thus lost to our national collections; but Dr. Atkinson,
in explanation of this seemingly long delay, said that he was satisfied that the
256 articles were *primâ facie* Treasure Trove, and that as such they would surely be
brought to the Academy for valuation and for subsequent deposit in its custody, that
771 he did not believe that Treasure found under such circumstances could be properly
purchased by anyone: and that, in fact, he had no knowledge of the purchase
260 actually made by the British Museum (in April 1897) until the beginning of 1898.
With regard to the value of the objects Dr. Atkinson stated that the Academy might
264 have given 200*l*. or 250*l*. for them, but that on his initiative the Council would not
have offered any such sum as 600*l*.

Early in the Parliamentary Session of last year questions were asked and a discussion arose in the House of Commons, wherein it was on the one side stated that the hoard in question, when found, was Treasure Trove; that the claim of the Crown to it as such had not been defeated by anything which had afterwards happened, and it was argued that the Treasure ought therefore to be recovered by the Government and handed over to the Royal Irish Academy; while on the other side it was contended that, apart from other objections to such a course, the authorities of the British Museum were precluded by the Statutes which govern that Institution from parting with such possessions even were they so minded. We shall not express any opinion upon the merits of this controversy, as the terms of your Lordships' Reference do not invite us to do so. 218.

We have to add that Mr. Day, on April 13th, 1898, wrote to the Chancellor of the Exchequer that he was willing to repay the Trustees of the British Museum £600 if they would transfer to him the ornaments in question, which he would hand over to the Royal Irish Academy on their reimbursing him. This offer, however, was withdrawn by Mr. Day on the 19th of May 1898, and the objects remain in the British Museum. 180, 181.

II.—"To consider and suggest regulations for avoiding undue competition between museums supported out of public funds in Scotland and Ireland on the one hand, and the British Museum on the other, for the acquisition of objects of antiquarian or historic interest; and for ensuring that in the case of objects which from their origin or associations are of peculiar interest either to Scotland or Ireland, the museum situated in the country so interested should be afforded an opportunity of purchasing them before they are acquired by any other institutions supported out of public funds." Reference.

We are of opinion that, should it at any time be deemed advisable to make regulations for the purposes set forth in the second paragraph of your Lordships' Reference, such regulations should be framed so as to provide that whenever it specially comes to the knowledge of the officers of any one of these institutions that objects which, from their origin or associations, appear to be of peculiar value to either of the others, have been offered, or are likely to be offered for sale, information to that effect should at once be conveyed to the body so specially interested, with the view of its having the first opportunity of purchasing such objects, and that, in order to avoid as far as possible the chance of undue competition, a friendly understanding should be arrived at as to what would be a reasonable price to give for the articles in question. These regulations might be framed for their own use by the Trustees of the British Museum and by the authorities of the other Institutions respectively. But due care ought to be taken, both in the drafting and enforcing of such regulations, to provide against the risk, by delay in concluding a bargain or otherwise, of the desired objects being lost to all three Museums.

We have, however, to report that the utmost good-will has generally prevailed between the authorities of the British Museum on the one hand and those of the Museums of Edinburgh and Dublin on the other, that the former have on several occasions zealously assisted in securing for the latter objects which seemed to have a preponderating value for their collections, and further that setting aside the very exceptional circumstances of the recent discovery in the North of Ireland with which we have already dealt, your Committee have found only one instance in which such undue competition as is contemplated in your Lordships' Minute has been made matter of complaint. That was the purchase by the British Museum of the "Glenlyon Brooch," an object long associated with a Scottish family, the Campbells of Troup, which the Council of the Society of Scottish Antiquaries were most anxious to obtain; but the evidence we have taken leads us to the conclusion that the contention in that case arose mainly if not altogether out of a misunderstanding between Mr. Read and Mr. Carfrae, the Agents who represented the British and the Scottish Museums respectively at the auction. Sir Edward Maunde Thompson told us that if the matter had been brought up for consideration in sufficient time beforehand he would have advised the Trustees of the British Museum to give way, while Mr. Read stated that if he had known that Mr. Carfrae was prepared to bid a sufficient sum to secure the brooch he would have taken the responsibility of retiring from the competition, and we think it not unlikely that the desired object might even after the sale have been returned to Scotland, had not the Statutes which govern the British Museum made such a proceeding impossible. 13, 131, 181, 383, 411, 575, 158; 48–50, 58–60, 139, 548, 520–595, 610, 612; 58; 108

The policy indicated in the paragraph of your Lordships' Minute now under consideration has been to some extent challenged by gentlemen who gave evidence before us, but we are satisfied, having regard to the friendly relations which have with such slight interruption existed between the authorities of the three National Museums, that if that policy were accepted by them in the spirit which has hitherto in the main so happily prevailed, effect could well be given to it by their spontaneous co-operation.

III.—"To consider whether any, and if so what, relaxations should be made in the regulations (statutory or otherwise) which prevent the British Museum parting with objects which it has once acquired."

In answer to the third paragraph of your Lordships' Reference, we beg to say that the majority of the witnesses heard by us were in favour of relaxing to some extent the statutory provisions which prevent the British Museum from parting with objects which it has acquired (unless such objects are duplicates or are deemed by the Trustees unfit for remaining in the Collection) and we recommend that the necessary steps should be taken for that purpose; but we think that the conditions under which the Trustees should be enabled to dispose of any property of which they are thus possessed ought to be very carefully considered, and we would suggest that such relaxation might perhaps be confined to cases in which the Trustees may in their discretion be willing to transfer, by way of exchange or otherwise, some article in their possession to one of the other National Museums.

We venture further to recommend that corresponding relaxations should also be made in the rules which now impose on the National Museums of Ireland and Scotland restrictions similar to those above mentioned as controlling the British Museum under its Statutes, and that in all cases such transfers should be sanctioned at a general meeting of the Trustees, or of the Councils of the Royal Irish Academy, and the Society of Antiquaries of Scotland respectively.

In conclusion, we desire to express our sense of the valuable services rendered to us by Mr. E. G. Harman and Mr. L. J. Hewby, who have successively acted as Secretaries to this Committee.

RATHMORE.
JOHN MORLEY.
JOHN LUBBOCK.
JOHN EVANS.
HERBERT MAXWELL.
THOS. H. GRATTAN ESMONDE.

L. J. Hewby, *Secretary*.
5th April, 1899.

We have signed the above Report, with which we are in general agreement, but as regards Part II. we think that the initiative should be taken by the authorities of the Museum desiring to purchase any special object; and as regards Part III., though we admit that in some few cases the change suggested might be desirable, we think that the balance of advantage rests with the present system. If, however, any change be made, we accept the provisions suggested in the Report.

JOHN LUBBOCK.
JOHN EVANS.

LIST OF WITNESSES.

Sir Edward Maunde Thompson, K.C.B., &c.

Mr C. H. Read, F.S.A.

Professor R. Atkinson, LL.D.

Mr G. Coffey

The Viscount Dillon, P.S.A.

Sir J. C. Robinson, F.S.A.

Dr David Christison

Mr R. Cochrane

Colonel G. T. Plunkett

COMMITTEE

ON

THE RELATIONS BETWEEN THE BRITISH MUSEUM

AND THE

MUSEUMS OF DUBLIN AND EDINBURGH.

FIRST DAY.

PALACE OF WESTMINSTER.

Wednesday, 7th December, 1898.

PRESENT:

The Right Hon. The Lord RAYLEIGH (*Chairman*).

Sir T. GRATTAN ESMONDE, Bart., M.P.
Sir JOHN EVANS, K.C.B.

The Right Hon. Sir Herbert E. MAXWELL, Bart., M.P.
The Right Hon. JOHN MORLEY, M.P.

E. G. HARMAN, Esq. (*Secretary*).
C. J. HEWBY, Esq. (*Acting Secretary*).

Sir EDWARD MAUNDE THOMPSON, K.C.B., D.C.L., LL.D., F.S.A., called; and Examined.

Sir E. M. Thompson, K.C.B., D.C.L., LL.D., F.S.A.

7 Dec. 1898.

1. (*Chairman.*) You are Director and Principal Librarian of the British Museum?—Yes.

2. You have been connected with the British Museum for nearly 40 years?—Since 1861.

3. As regards the matter which this Committee has to consider, will you tell us the circumstances under which the British Museum acquired possession of these gold ornaments?—I have drawn up the following memorandum:—"In the autumn of 1896, Mr Robert Day, F.S.A., a well known collector of works of art and antiquities living in Cork, informed Mr C. H. Read, the keeper of the British and Mediaeval Antiquities in the British Museum, that he had secured from a silversmith some very fine gold ornaments of the late Celtic work. Mr Read, who is also the Secretary of the Society of Antiquaries of London, suggested to Mr Day that the society should have an opportunity of seeing them. Accordingly Mr Day exhibited the ornaments at a meeting of the society, on the 14th January 1897, and an account of the meeting appeared in the *Athenaeum* newspaper of the 30th January.

Meanwhile Mr Read having expressed an opinion to Mr Day that these important objects should pass to the British Museum, should he at any time part with them, negotiations followed, with the result that Mr Day offered the collection to the Trustees of the British Museum for the sum of 600*l.*

Mr Read recommended the purchase to the Trustees in a report of the 5th April 1897, a copy of which is hereto annexed.

The Trustees sanctioned the purchase at a meeting of the Standing Committee on the 8th April 1897. The order for payment was issued on the 13th May." Would the Committee like to hear the report of Mr Read to the Trustees?

4. If you please?—This is the report: "British Museum, Department of British Antiquities, &c., 5th day of April 1897." "Mr Read has the honour to request the sanction of the Standing Committee to make the following important purchase, as soon as such a portion of the grant shall become available, viz.:—

From Robert Day, Esq., F.S.A.—A find of gold ornaments of the late Celtic period (about 100 A.D.) from the North-West of Ireland, for 600*l.*

This discovery is probably the most important that has ever been made of objects of this very interesting period, a period in which the Museum is exceptionally rich, though the examples in the precious metals are by no means numerous. The find consists of the following objects:—

1. A hollow collar in two sections with elaborate repoussé ornament of curvilinear curves, &c., which are a distinctive character of this art.

2. A model of a boat with eight thwarts (originally nine), and a number of oars, spars, &c.

3. A hemispherical bowl of thin metal with four rings at the edges for suspension.

4. A solid gold torc of stout wire with a thinner wire twisted round it.

5. One half of a similar torc.

6. A necklace formed of three plaited chains with a peculiar fastening.

7. A thin single chain necklace of the same plaiting.

All these objects are stated to have been found together by a man ploughing in the North-West of Ireland, and were secured soon afterwards by Mr Day, a well-known collector, of Cork, who verified the account on the spot. Mr Day at first had a much higher opinion of the money value of his hoard, but finally offered them at 750*l.* This sum he has now consented to reduce to 600*l.*, at which price Mr Read would strongly recommend the purchase.—*Charles H. Read.*"

5. Was there not an article published in the *Athenaeum* upon this subject?—That was afterwards.

6. After the purchase?—After the purchase, later in the year, in the summer.

7. Did you have any communication from the Royal Irish Academy or any authority in Ireland on this subject before the purchase was effected?—None whatever.

8. I understand from the proceedings in Parliament on this subject that it was contended in the House of Commons, on behalf of the British Museum, that it would have been impossible for them to part with these articles, because the Act of Parliament which governs the British Museum in this respect precludes them from

Sir E. M. Thompson, K.C.B., D.C.L., LL.D., F.S.A.

7 Dec 1898

parting with them?—There are certain modifications of the first Act of Incorporation of 1753 by which we are forbidden to part with anything. Perhaps I might explain the modifications under the different Acts since that time. The 7 George III., c. 18, is "An Act to enable the Trustees of the British Museum to exchange, sell, or dispose of, any duplicates of printed books, medals, coins, or other curiosities; and for laying out the money arising by such sale in the purchase of other things that may be wanting in, or proper for, the said Museum." Then the 47 George III., c. 36, is "An Act to enable the Trustees of the British Museum to exchange, sell, or dispose of such parts of the collections, and under such restrictions as are therein specified." That Act was not confined to duplicates. The Preamble says: "Whereas amongst the several collections and additions thereto, which from time to time have been and may be placed in the British Museum, there now are and hereafter may happen to be some articles which are unfit to be preserved therein." That was the point of that Act. If articles are found to be "unfit" to be preserved, then we can part with them.

9. How do you understand that word in the Act, "unfit"?—It is governed in a certain way by the occasion. I will give you an instance that occurred a short time ago. We bought amongst a collection of Oriental manuscripts one single leaf of a Sanskrit manuscript. Naturally we purchase everything of the sort that we think ought to be preserved, and we purchased this and kept it, but afterwards it was found that that leaf belonged to a manuscript in the India Office. Having ascertained its real position, the trustees decided that that leaf was "unfit" to be kept in our collection, and was more fit to be kept with the manuscript in the India Office.

10. (*Mr John Morley.*) A mutilated manuscript would come under the heading "unfit"?—In the same way we might consider a mercenary unfit, in which case we should dispose of it as we could. Then there is another Act, the 41 and 42 Vict., c. 55. Section 3 of that Act is, "The trustees of the British Museum may also give away any duplicate works, objects, or specimens not required for the purposes of the Museum: Provided always, that the power hereby conferred shall not extend to any duplicate works in the Royal Library of King George the Fourth, or in the Cracherode, Grenville, or Banksian Libraries, or to any objects presented to the Museum for use and preservation therein."

11. (*Chairman.*) That is still limited to duplicates?—"Any duplicate works, objects, or specimens"; it is not exchanging or selling, but giving them away.

12. But still, any duplicates?—Yes.

13. (*Mr T. Kennedy.*) What was the Act under which you transferred that manuscript to the India Office?—That was under the 47 Geo. III., c. 36.

14. (*Chairman.*) I understand that your view is that these particular Irish articles would not be governed by either of these exceptions?—No.

15. And that, therefore, you consider that under your Act of Parliament you would have no power to restore them unless there was some alteration made by legislation?—Just so.

16. You know that the Attorney-General for Ireland has stated in the House of Commons that, so far as he had been able to form an opinion on the subject, these articles were considered as treasure trove?—Yes.

17. And I dare say you know that a contention has been raised that, in point of fact, the Crown has a superior title to that which was acquired by the British Museum by purchase, and that it would be possible for the Crown to assert such a title if it were so disposed?—Yes.

18. I do not ask you to express any opinion upon that, of course, but if such a title were asserted by the Crown, and the British Museum were satisfied that it was legally and properly asserted, there would be no difficulty in restoring these articles, so far as you know the Trustees of the Museum would have no hesitation in restoring them to the Crown?—I presume that the Trustees would not have any choice in the matter.

19. You know there was a Bill introduced into the House of Commons last Session by Mr Redmond which was objected to, I believe, by the authorities of the British Museum on various grounds?—Yes.

20. Will you be good enough to read the operative part of that Bill?—You refer to the Antiquities (Ireland) (Transfer) Bill, 1898, which was "A Bill to enable the transfer of certain Irish antiquities from the British Museum to the National Museum, Dublin. Be it enacted by the Queen's Most Excellent Majesty, by and with the advice and consent of the Lords Spiritual and Temporal, and Commons in this present Parliament assembled, and by the authority of the same, as follows:—1. This Act may be cited as the British Museum Act, 1898. 2. This Act may be read and construed together as one with the British Museum Act, 1878. 3. The Trustees of the British Museum may, with the consent of the Lords Commissioners of Her Majesty's Treasury, remove any of the collections in their possession or custody, or any of them, or any part thereof, to the Royal Irish Academy, Dublin (known as the National Museum, Dublin), there to remain and be preserved by the Council of the said Academy for public use to all posterity."

21. (*Sir J. Evans.*) What was the Act of 1878 to which that refers?—That was the one about duplicates, that we could dispose of duplicates. The Act was the 41 & 42 Vict. c. 55.

22. (*Chairman.*) The British Museum, I think, objected to that Bill being passed at that time. Will you state to us, so far as you know, what the objections were?—The objection was that it was so very wide to begin with. Anything might come under it. The whole British Museum might be placed on College Green, I take it.

23. But, apart from that general objection, you objected to it for specific reasons?—On both grounds.

24. (*Sir J. Evans.*) It was also too narrow; it did not provide for transfers to the Scottish Museum?—The question of Ireland was before us at the moment.

25. (*Chairman.*) You say it was too large in its scope?—Yes.

26. What was your general objection?—The Bill proposed that the Trustees should "remove any of the collections in their possession or custody, or any of them or any part thereof, to the Royal Irish Academy, Dublin." It is so very wide. It was not defined.

27. It would only have enabled you to do so?—Of course; but we did not see that in this particular case the Trustees were called upon to give away these things.

28. (*Mr John Morley.*) It does not limit it to objects of special interest to Ireland?—Not at all. It is as wide as it can be.

29. (*Sir J. Evans.*) Did not the Trustees pass some resolution on the subject? Perhaps you had better read that.—The Bill was objected to, and the question has since been referred, in accordance with an undertaking of the First Lord of the Treasury, to this Committee. The Trustees of the Museum, to whom the Bill was referred, reported their opinion that Mr Redmond's Bill, "while in one sense very narrow in its scope, raises a very large question, and is in entire opposition to the principles which have hitherto been adopted in reference to the national collections, and that if the law which defines the Trustees' obligations with regard to those collections is to be altered, it should be only after careful consideration of the question in all its bearings, and on the initiative of Her Majesty's Government."

30. (*Chairman.*) That raises a point as to which I was about to ask you a question. Apart from the particular case of these gold ornaments, have you had previously in your experience any case of competition between the British Museum and the Royal Irish Academy or any other Irish museum for articles of interest?—I do not remember any.

31. (*Sir Herbert Maxwell.*) Do you limit that to Ireland?

32. (*Chairman.*) Yes, I am at present limiting it to Ireland?—I do not remember any case of competition.

33. This is hardly a case of competition?—Well, I will say a case of claim. Here is a minute that I will read: "At a Committee, 11th June 1870. Read a letter, dated the 8th of June, from Mr Birch, enclosing one from the Rev. M. H. Close, of Dublin, applying on behalf of the Royal Irish Academy for possession of a Bronze [illegible] said to have been found near Dublin about twenty-five years ago and sold to the British Museum by Miss Walsh in 1851 for [illegible]. Mr Close offered to purchase the [illegible] from the Trustees. Ordered, That Mr Close be informed that the Trustees cannot accede to his application." That is the only case of any claim from Ireland as far as I know.

34. (*Mr John Morley.*) And it dropped there?—It dropped there.

35 (*Sir T. Esmonde.*) May I ask before we leave the subject, would you have objected to Mr Redmond's Bill if it had been specifically limited to these gold ornaments?—Yes, I think so, certainly

36 You objected on general grounds?—We objected on the general ground that the Trustees had not power to transfer the articles.

37 The Bill would have dealt with that objection, because it would have given you power; but would you have objected if it had referred to these ornaments alone?—Yes, because we consider that these ornaments are very valuable for the British Museum.

38 (*Chairman.*) I think that is all I need ask you about the Irish case. Have you had any controversy or competition with the Society of Antiquaries in Scotland?—Yes

39 I mean besides the Glenlyon Brooch case?—I was going to cite that.

40 But besides that have you had any other instance of any claim on the part of Scotland?—I think there was one. On the 20th February, 1863, the Lord Clerk Register of Scotland asked that certain manuscripts we had, which were alleged to have been part of the public records of Scotland, might be transferred to the General Register House in Edinburgh, but the Trustees refused.

41 Were there any grounds stated for the refusal?—I will read you the minute:—"At a Committee, 28th February 1863,

Read a letter dated 20th February from the Lord Clerk Register of Scotland, asking that certain manuscripts purchased for the British Museum, and alleged, in the letter, to have been part of the public records of Scotland, might be transferred to the General Register House in Edinburgh, either by way of sale or exchange, or as a deposit, to be returned to the British Museum when required

A copy of a memorandum descriptive of the manuscripts, which accompanied the Lord Clerk's letter, was laid before the Board, together with a letter from Sir Frederic Madden" (Sir F. Madden was Keeper of the manuscripts), "dated 27th February, which was read

Ordered,—That the Deputy Principal Librarian acquaint the Lord Clerk Register of Scotland that the Trustees are quite willing to allow the manuscripts in question to be copied for the use of the General Register House in Edinburgh, but that they would not be justified in parting with the originals, which have been purchased for the Museum, or in transferring them to any other custody than that of their own officers."

42 That is, I presume, relying on the Act of Parliament to which you have already referred?—Yes

43 I may tell you that we have been furnished with a letter which was written on behalf of the Society of Antiquaries in Scotland, and signed by Dr David Christison, the secretary,* in which it is stated, referring to the terms of the reference to this Committee, or to that part which deals with undue competition, "It may be stated that up to quite recently no such undue competition as is here referred to had ever taken place between the British Museum and the National Museum of Antiquities under the charge of the Society. It had formerly been the practice of the Society when desirous of acquiring for the Museum any object of special antiquarian interest to Scotland that may have come into the market to intimate their desire to the British Museum, when the claim of the Scottish Museum was courteously recognised, and competition was avoided." That is their statement. Do you recall any instance in which representations of that kind had been made prior to the Glenlyon brooch case?—I do not remember such a case

44 I presume such an arrangement might be made by the keepers of Departments without the matter coming before you?—Of course it is always understood that there is common courtesy between Museums. If a Scottish or Irish museum or a provincial museum puts forward a claim or states that it wishes to purchase a particular thing that is in the market, the British Museum always meets the request in every possible way; the representation is always listened to

45 (*Sir Herbert Maxwell.*) Do you call the Edinburgh and Dublin museums provincial?—Perhaps that is a wrong term; I will say "national"

46 (*Chairman.*) You say it is always listened to, but what is the result of the statement that you give to these applications?—If they make out that the object is really wanted for Ireland or Scotland, and that they have a superior claim, we should at once give way; we should not bid

47 You mean you do not step forward as purchasers?—Just so. I see that a similar application was made on the 11th June, 1864 from the Lord Clerk Register about these particular manuscripts, and that was again refused. There is nothing else.

48 Now will you tell us what happened as regards the Glenlyon brooch?—At the time that the Glenlyon brooch matter turned up, I had a memorandum drawn up by the Keeper of the Department concerned, Mr. Read, which gives the whole story. I had better read it:—

"17th June, 1887.

"*Memorandum for the Principal Librarian*

"With regard to the memorial from the Scottish Museum on the subject of the Glenlyon brooch, I should like first to point out that, so far as it concerns my conduct in the affair, it leaves a wrong impression

"As you know, I recommended the purchase to the Trustees in a report dated 1st May, asking permission to buy the brooch up to 200*l*. This being granted, I think my duty was clearly to secure it unless it went much beyond that sum. In my opinion, as shown by my report, the Memorial is not justified in speaking of £230 as a high price, it being only 10 per cent. above my estimate

"The circumstances immediately preceding the sale are these. Mr Carfrae, representing the Scottish Museum, called upon me on the morning of the sale and requested me not to bid for the brooch. I explained to him my position, and finally suggested, as a means of avoiding competition, that he should tell me his limit of price and I would then show him my recommendation to the Trustees. He declined to accede to this and stated that he would see me in the sale room. He did so see me, but confined himself to a request that I should withdraw altogether; but this, as I explained, I could not with propriety do. His words then were, 'Very well, then, we must fight for it.' Finally, when the brooch was put up, I understand that competition from about 120*l*. onwards was entirely between a private buyer and myself. Thus, had I withdrawn in favour of the Scottish Antiquaries, the brooch would have been lost to the nation

"I think it well to mention that there were several other Scottish objects sold at the same time as the brooch, including the Glenlyon Crystal, and that although I did not bid for any of these, they realised prices that in Mr Carfrae's opinion, as stated to me, were far too high. It would appear, therefore, that my competition was not needed to make these Scottish objects fetch good prices

"On the general question of the importance of the brooch for the Museum, my report of the 1st May refers to it as an important acquisition, and this it undoubtedly is. I am glad to be able to state that I had the opportunity of showing it to my late chief, Sir A. Wollaston Franks, who fully confirmed my opinion of its value and recommended its purchase to me. Such objects, whether Scottish or not, are becoming very scarce, and I should have been disposed to buy it as an interesting example of its kind and period. The fact of its being from the British Islands undoubtedly makes it a more desirable purchase for the British Museum

"We have naturally, and quite properly, a certain number of Scottish objects in the Museum, and I trust that these in due time will bear a proper relation to those from England and Ireland, so that the archaeology of the Empire may be properly represented in the National Museum. One of the best known objects is, curiously enough, also a brooch—the Lochbuy brooch—a very interesting object, obtained at the sale of the Bernal Collection

"It would appear that the Glenlyon brooch was not at first considered of great importance for the Scottish Museum. Mr Carfrae was informed of the sale some time before it took place, and Messrs Christie's catalogues are issued by them at least a week before the sale. It is therefore scarcely accurate—as stated in the memorial—that there was only 'a few days' in which to make application to the Treasury. Mr Carfrae must have had knowledge of the coming sale at least a week—and more probably a fortnight—before it took place."

49 (*Chairman.*) Let me suggest a point in passing. Do you see that if Mr Carfrae, who represented the Scottish body, was aware that the British Museum intended to bid against him, he may possibly have been

Sir E. M. Thompson, K.C.B., D.C.L., LL.D., F.S.A.

7 Dec 1898

* See Appendix II

Sir E. M. Thompson, K.C.B., D.C.L., LL.D., F.S.A.

7 Dec 1898

thereby induced not to bid against the private purchaser. He might say "It is no use my bidding against this private purchaser if after I have done with him I have to deal with the British Museum?"—I have heard since (I do not know whether it is absolutely the fact) that the second bidder dropped out and that it was the Scottish Antiquaries who were going against us. How that is I do not know, but I think I may be allowed to say in this case that it was a misjudgment of Mr. Carfrae's not to disclose his price. He came at the last moment, and when he was asked to disclose his price he declined to do so.

50. (*Mr. John Morley*) If Mr. Read declined to disclose his price why should Mr Carfrae disclose his?—He was asked first of all.

51. (*Chairman*) Now I want to call your attention to this. Whether they came rather late in the field is another matter, but this was clearly a case in which the Scottish Society of Antiquaries did desire to obtain this article for their collection in Scotland, and apart from the question that we have just been discussing as to the particular form in which the request was made, as to disclosing the prices and so on, does it not raise the general question which is afterwards stated in Mr Read's memorandum that you have read to us, whether in the future the British Museum is to perfect its collection of what they call British specimens, whether the Scottish National Museum desires to get them first or not? I put that to you because you have stated to us that it has always been your practice up to the present, whenever a Scottish body [illegible] a desire to obtain a Scottish object for its collection, that as a matter of courtesy you did not enter into competition with them. There may be special circumstances in this particular case about which you came to a certain decision, but the serious point that Mr. Read raises is, that it is his intention, as far as possible, to gather these things into the British Museum even though they have a special interest for Scotland?—I do not think you can carry it so far as that. If the Scottish antiquaries stated that this was absolutely a thing that they ought to have in Scotland, I think we should defer to that opinion; but they ought not to prevent us buying Scottish antiquities at all, because there may be many Scottish antiquities which the Society of Antiquaries may not care to have, but which we might care to have. We ought to be quite at liberty to buy them, surely.

52. But the point which I think we shall have to consider by and bye is, whether it should not be a practice, if not a rule, that whenever the British Museum has an opportunity of buying Scottish or Irish specimens, or whenever the British Museum becomes cognisant of the fact that there are specimens in the market which may be of interest to Scotland or Ireland, notice should be given to the museum representing the country specially interested?—You mean notice from the British Museum?

53. Yes, or from the others to you as the case may be?—That is, I think, for the Committee to decide.

54. Therefore I ask you this question. Supposing that such a notice were given, and that the body to whom the notice was given went to intimate, as they did in this Glenlyon case, though perhaps at a rather late period of the affair, that they desired to purchase the article for their own collection if they could, are we to understand from you that in that case, notwithstanding what Mr. Read says in his memorandum, you would stand aside and let them buy it if they could?—Certainly, I think so. Of course you have to take this into consideration, that we should have to examine their claim, and if we could show that the thing was of equal importance for the British Museum to have, it would, of course, be a matter of negotiation.

55. That is to say you mean if the Scottish or the Irish body were not able to establish the claim that the article had a special national interest for their body?—Just so.

56. (*Sir T. Esmonde*) Of course the British Museum has its own interests which you are primarily bound to look after?—Certainly, it represents the Empire. It is not a London Museum, it is not an English Museum, it is a "British Museum," and as such we naturally have to look after its interests, and make our collection as perfect as possible, to represent every portion of the British Empire. As I have just explained, in the case of a strong claim being put in by Dublin or Edinburgh, it would be considered, and if we were perfectly satisfied that there was what I may call a national claim we should give way.

57. But you would be rather inclined first to consider the claims of the British Museum?—Certainly, but not as overriding everything else. Of course it is a matter of negotiation.

58. (*Chairman*) But I should like to have your opinion, if you will kindly give it us, upon this particular case of the Glenlyon brooch?—I think I may say that if the matter had been brought up properly before us beforehand, we should have given way—I think so. I am only speaking, of course, my own opinion at the moment, but certainly I should have advised the Trustees to give way on this point. But as a matter of fact Mr Carfrae came at the last moment, and, if I may be allowed to say so, he was perhaps a little singular.

59. (*Mr. John Morley*) You consider that there was—I will try to use the least offensive word—some misunderstanding or mismanagement at the moment of negotiation?—That is what I take it to be. I have always looked upon it as a case of misjudgment at the moment.

60. (*Chairman*) And the thing once being done you could not under your Act of Parliament get away from it?—Just so.

61. Now one of the things this Committee has to do is to consider and "suggest regulations for avoiding undue competition between museums supported out of public funds." Are there any regulations existing at present other than what may be called a custom other than the regulations of the Act of Parliament?—There is a regulation between us and the South Kensington Museum. I am afraid I have not got the document here. In 1883 I think there was a series of regulations drawn up in order to prevent the South Kensington Museum bidding (I think it was particularly) for classical antiquities. I think that was the matter it turned upon.

62. Was that in the nature of an agreement between the two bodies?—No. As far as my recollection goes it was a minute drawn up at South Kensington under the Science and Art Department.

63. That would be regulating the South Kensington Museum, not the British Museum?—It was in relation to us. It was to prevent them bidding for classical antiquities, if I recollect rightly, which of course ought to come to the Museum.

64. Will you kindly supply us with that document?—Yes, I will send you a copy.*

65. Then, apart from that, can you tell us any regulation other than the regulation of the Acts of Parliament which govern you?—No.

66. Have the Trustees of the Museum from time to time drawn up any rules upon this subject?—I do not remember any.

67. Would you mind reading me the terms of the first Act of Parliament which gives you your general authority and discretion?—It is the Act of 1753, the 26th Geo. II, c. 22. It was an Act for the purchase of Sir Hans Sloane's collection, that is how the Museum began. The 10th section is: "Provided always that the said Museum or collection of Sir Hans Sloane in all its branches shall be kept and preserved together in the said general repository whole and entire."

68. (*Mr. John Morley*) It is an Act constituting the body of Trustees, vesting powers in them and providing them with funds?—Yes.

69. (*Chairman*) Will you give us the words vesting powers in the Trustees so far as this particular matter is concerned. We should like to know the exact powers that are given to them?—First of all, Section [illegible] says this: "Be it further enacted by the authority aforesaid, that the Archbishop of Canterbury," and so on, then it gives the number of official trustees and gives them power to elect fifteen others. Then Section 8 is, "And be it enacted by the authority aforesaid, that within the Cities of London or Westminster, or the suburbs thereof, one general repository shall be erected or provided in such convenient place, and in such manner as the Trustees hereby appointed, or the major part of them in a general meeting assembled, shall direct, for the reception not only of the said Museum, or Collection of Sir Hans Sloane, but also of the Cottonian Library, and of the additions which have been or shall be made thereunto by virtue of the last will and testament of the said Arthur Edwards, and likewise of the said Harleian Collection of manuscripts, and of such other additions to the Cottonian Library, as

* See 318, 319 where this document is quoted.

Sir E. M. Thompson, K.C.B., D.C.L., LL.D., F.S.A.

7 Dec 1908.

with the approbation of the Trustees by this Act appointed, or the major part of them at a general meeting assembled, shall be made thereunto, in manner hereafter mentioned, and of such other collections and libraries as with the like approbation shall be admitted into the said general repository, which several collections, additions, and libraries so received into the said general repository, shall remain to be preserved therein for public use to all posterity." That is the point I think you want.

70. No, that is not the point; that is recited in the subsequent Act; but what I want to know is with what authority are the Trustees clothed. Is there any authority to make regulations?—Yes.

71. I want to know the scope of their authority?—First of all in Section 4 certain persons are named who "shall be Trustees for putting this Act in execution and they or the major part of them in any general meeting assembled"—then it goes on to provide for the election of fifteen more. That is a general power.

72. But I suppose you have no doubt that under their powers they could if they chose have framed regulations which would have put on record the practice which you have referred to as existing?—Yes, they can make any regulations they please.

73. I mean such regulations so that there shall be a reciprocal notice given such as I have referred to to secure the reciprocal security that they should not compete against one another?—Yes.

74. Then I want to call your attention to a rather important paragraph at the end of the letter from the Society of Antiquaries of Scotland, from which I have already quoted a passage or two. They say at the end: "As to the third reference whether any, and, if so, what relaxations should be made in the regulations, statutory or otherwise, which prevent the British Museum parting with objects which it has once acquired. The Society thinks it highly desirable, with the view of making each of the three Museums thoroughly representative of its own area, that they should be empowered to transfer objects of exceptional antiquarian or historic interest to the National Museum of the area to which their exceptional interest specially appertains." That goes rather beyond anything that we have been talking of up to the present. We have been dealing rather with the future in these particular cases, but this is apparently a suggestion that it would be desirable to have some regulation—or I suppose it would have to be an Act of Parliament really—to overcome the Act which at present exists to the contrary—a new Act of Parliament which would enable you to part with articles already in the British Museum to these National Museums?—An Act would be absolutely necessary; we have no power whatever under our present Acts.

75. Suppose it were thought desirable to adopt the suggestion, do you see any probable injury or inconvenience from the point of view of the British Museum?—I should say so, most decidedly.

76. Will you explain your views as to that?—It would open the door so very wide. We might have to go back a long way. Of course there would be a large question then in regard to all the collections that we have acquired year after year as to how far they would be affected by this Act. I think it would lead to endless trouble.

77. Is there a very large number of such articles at present in the British Museum—articles which might possibly be desired by the National Museums of Ireland and Scotland as more particularly appropriate to their keeping?—That opens a very large question. Of course, if you go back to the early times, what we call the Celtic art is not confined to Ireland or to Scotland. It extends all over England, and even to the Continent. Therefore, in the case, for example, of these particular Irish ornaments, there is no reason on earth why they should have been made in Ireland; they might very well have been made in England.

78. (*Sir Herbert Maxwell.*) In the case of the Glenlyon brooch, that is Scottish?—That is Scottish. There, of course, we know what we are; but if you once opened the door to deciding what particular country an article is specially appropriate to, you would lead to endless trouble.

(*Sir John Evans.*) It might turn out to be a question between James I. of England and James VI. of Scotland.

79. (*Chairman.*) Now, what are the relations of the British Museum with Parliament or the Treasury as regards your subvention?—To go back to the beginning of things, the Act from which I have already made some quotations raised a fund for the British Museum by a lottery; 300,000*l.* was raised, 200,000*l.* of which was given in prizes, and 100,000*l.* came to the Museum. After paying for the Harleian collection and the Sloane collection and purchasing Montagu House, which is now the British Museum, a sum of 30,000*l.* was left, which was invested, and that remains to the present day invested in the Funds, and is all our endowment. But every year a petition is presented to Parliament asking for an increase of that endowment, and that Vote at the present time amounts to about [illegible]*l.*

80. That is an annual Vote?—That is so.

81. (*Mr. John Morley.*) Does the British Museum petition Parliament for that?—Yes. Sir John Lubbock always presents the petition. We seal it at our meeting, and he presents it.

82. (*Sir Herbert Maxwell.*) Leaving apart the question of the price of original manufacture of these gold ornaments or other objects, would you see any objection, in the future, to the national museums of Edinburgh and Dublin having the right of pre-emption of objects found in their respective countries?—Do you mean that we are to be excluded entirely from bidding without their leave first, or without their knowledge first?

83. In my question I did not define the right of pre-emption, but the idea is sufficiently clear—that the authorities of the museums in Dublin and Edinburgh should have the first chance of purchasing objects of interest—I do not mean all objects, but objects of special interest—found in their respective territories?—Personally, I see no objection whatever to that. I am only speaking from my own view of it.

84. You will admit, I presume, that it is undesirable that there should be competition?—I quite agree; but on the other hand may I say, on this question as to whether we should receive or give notice, it really comes to this. Perhaps one or two little mistakes have been made from the mere fact of the Keepers of the Museums of Scotland and Ireland not looking out quite sharp enough after these acquisitions. For instance, take the case of the Glenlyon brooch; that was a clear case of misjudgment. If they had warned us in the proper way we should of course have listened to them in a moment. In the same way with regard to these Celtic ornaments, if the Royal Irish Academy had come forward we should have listened to what they had to say. We do not want to enter into competition in these things.

85. But is it the case, is it not, that the Scottish Antiquaries are very much hampered by want of funds?—What I mean is, that they did not come forward till the last minute.

86. There were only ten days, I think, in which they could have come forward?—Do not you think the Glenlyon brooch was known in Scotland more than ten days? If I may say so, I think it is the duty of the keeper of a museum to look after the interests of his museum, and not quite to go to sleep and then wake up and find another museum has got something that he wanted, and then come forward and say, "What on earth do you mean by buying that?"

87. But you admit that negotiations were attempted?—Yes, but it was so late that there was no room for negotiation.

88. Is Mr. Carlow the authorised agent of the Society of Scottish Antiquaries?—I think Mr. Read will explain that better to you; but there is every wish on our part to act with the keepers of other museums.

89. Then as to the question of any degree of retrospective transfer, I understand you object to any relaxation of the regulations binding the Trustees?—I think our Act is a perfect Act, and the powers we have are quite reasonable.

90. *Beati possidentes?*—Exactly. I do not know where we should stop if that Act were relaxed and people were able to put in claims for all kinds of things.

91. Or proposals?—Proposals or claims.

92. For example, we have certain things in Edinburgh which your Trustees would, I imagine, be very glad to get for a consideration?—Yes.

93. Should there not be some method of arranging that?—It might be a matter of exchange. Then, of course, according to the present Acts, we should have to consider whether the object which was proposed to be exchanged—the object in our possession—was [illegible].

94. I am asking you whether you would object to

Mr. E. M. Thompson, K.C.B., D.C.L., LL.D., P.S.A.

7 Dec. [illegible]

discretionary powers being conferred on your trustees?—No, I have no personal objection.

95. (*Sir John Evans.*) Have you had any difficulty with South Kensington bidding against you or you bidding against them?—No, I do not remember any case, certainly not in recent years.

96. Do South Kensington act as agents for the Royal Irish Academy at sales in London?—The Royal Irish Museum is under the Science and Art Department now, I think.

97. I believe they are the acting officers?—Yes.

98. But the main point which occurs to me, as one on which we want some enlightenment, is this: you speak about being able to make regulations not to enter into competition. That, I presume, refers to public sales—sales by auction? Yes, mainly.

99. Do you see any possible regulation that would prevent the British Museum from entering into private negotiations for the purchase of anything?—No.

100. Would it be possible in the case of a private negotiation to refer the matter to Ireland or Scotland, and await the result?—Well, it depends entirely on the circumstances. It might be a matter of time; for instance, an offer might come in suddenly. A man may come with an article and say, "I want 400*l*.; if I have 400*l*. to-day you shall have the article; if not it will go to the Continent." It would then be our duty to buy it at once if we wanted it.

101. No regulation could be allowed to affect that?—No.

102. With regard to the general question, is not it extremely desirable that the national collection—which is really the British Museum—should have representative series both from Ireland and Scotland for comparison with those of England?—Decidedly.

103. You are strongly of that opinion?—Most decidedly, otherwise we should lose our position as a "British" museum and become an English museum.

104. Do you know of your own knowledge in whom the collections of Ireland are vested; is it vested in the nation, or does it belong to the Royal Irish Academy?—That I am not in a position to say. I should think, being under the Science and Art Department, it would belong to the nation.

107. I believe it is under their management, but not in their ownership?—I do not know exactly how that is.

108. (*Mr. John Morley.*) Referring to one of your answers to Sir John Evans, you do not accept, as a matter of principle, that when, for example, these Celtic ornaments were found in Ireland, and a strong Irish feeling was found to exist that they had better be placed in the Dublin Museum, you would not say that the unbridled instinct of the collector—in the case of a museum, armed with unlimited funds—is to prevail over these local sentiments, and that all these objects, if they are only local to the extent of being locally found, are to be swept up into the British Museum?—I did not gather that Sir John Evans was putting rather the extreme case that we ought to purchase the object, in order to prevent its being lost altogether.

107. (*Sir John Evans.*) If you defer a bargain indefinitely, while other people have to consider what they will give, the chances are in many cases that the bargain will fall through?—Naturally, we must not injure ourselves in that way. It would be absurd that the museum should be injured by having to allow time for other bodies to make up their mind. But Mr. Morley, I understand, is putting the broad principle to me, and I quite agree.

108. (*Mr. John Morley.*) You are not so enamoured by the idea of making your collection perfect as to feel yourself justified in depleting the National Museums of Ireland and Scotland by purchasing anything on which you can lay your hands?—Certainly not.

109. (*Sir John Evans.*) You have had arrangements with the Scottish Antiquaries, and I presume occasionally with the Royal Irish Academy with regard to the purchase of objects?—As to the Royal Irish Academy the only case I remember was in the matter of the Ashburnham Manuscripts. That was really a matter which the Government took up. All the Irish manuscripts in the collection went to the Royal Irish Academy.

110. (*Chairman.*) On the point raised by Sir John Evans just now as to whether the collection in Ireland is really a national one, I should like to ask you this. Under the Treasury Minute, dated the 8th November 1877, one of the conditions made by the Treasury in the negotiations with the Royal Irish Academy was: "The entire collection of antiquarian coins and medals belonging to the Royal Irish Academy, with such additions as may be hereafter made to them, and the cabinets, glass cases, &c. in which they are contained, to be conveyed to the Lords of the Committee of Council on Education to be retained in Ireland on behalf of the public." That is, I believe, copied from an analogous condition in the agreement entered into between the Treasury and the Scottish Museum. Therefore in both those cases whatever things are deposited in these national museums of Scotland and Ireland are to be retained there on behalf of the public?—Clearly.

111. (*Sir John Evans.*) In point of fact the collections vest in those bodies.

(*Chairman.*) They vest in those bodies to be retained for the public in perpetuity. Now, there is another question arising out of what you said just now. You told us, I think, that in the case of the Glenlyon brooch the ultimate result of the negotiations was that you said you were not able, under your Act of Parliament, to let them have the brooch itself, but you were able to provide them with a copy of that brooch, which copy, I believe, you contend is very difficult to distinguish from the original. In such a case as that, does it not occur to you that it would be convenient, in order to meet the national sentiment, which we know has a great deal to do with these questions, that the original should, if it were made possible by Act of Parliament, vest in or be deposited with the national museum of the country to which it belongs, and that an exact copy, such as you describe, would be sufficient for all practical purposes for the British Museum?—I do not know whether I ought to answer that question. I do not know whether you are asking me as Director of the Museum or as a private individual.

112. Let me ask you this further question; you need not answer it unless you like. Have you had any opportunity of discussing these matters at all with your Trustees before coming here? I mean, have you conferred with them on the views you have expressed to us?—Of course, I have gathered their views at the meetings of the standing committee.

113. Do you think there is anything in what you have said that they would be likely to object to?—Well, there are two members of the standing committee here.

114. But I mean you have given us some very important views as to the possibility of these matters being carried on in the future in a certain way?—Yes, I think I may say that I have expressed the views of the standing committee.

115. (*Sir John Evans.*) I think the standing committee has expressed its opinion very strongly with regard to that proposed Act of Parliament?

(*Sir Herbert Maxwell.*) That was with regard to that particular Bill.

116. (*Sir John Evans.*) I think their view was that the whole subject required further consideration from various points of view, and that is certainly still the opinion of the Trustees, I think.

(*Witness.*) The Trustees have always taken the strong ground that we must stand by the Statute.

117. (*Mr. John Morley.*) But surely the minute of the standing committee which you read, as Sir John Evans truly says, was to the effect that they could not stand the words of Mr. Redmond's Bill, but they did not regard the whole question as closed.

(*Sir John Evans.*) Oh, no.

118. (*Chairman.*) The words are, that the Bill "which is one upon very narrow in its scope, raises a very large question, and is in entire opposition to the principles which have hitherto been adopted in reference to the national collections, and that if the law which defines the Trustees' obligations in regard to those collections is to be altered it should be only after careful consideration of the question in all its bearings, and on the initiative of Her Majesty's Government." It was, in fact, upon that that this Committee was appointed.

(*Sir John Evans.*) The feeling would also be that if the law is to be altered it ought not to be altered merely to meet a particular case as this one.

119. (*Chairman.*) Do you gather that that is the view of the Trustees?—That I think is so.

120. (*Sir T. Esmonde.*) I presume Mr. Read will answer any questions of detail with regard to the matter of your statement put before us in evidence as to the Irish gold ornaments?—Yes, he is the keeper of the Department which conducted the negotiation.

Mr Charles Hercules Read, F.S.A., called, and Examined

121. (*Chairman.*) What is your position?—I am the Keeper of the Department of British and Mediæval Antiquities and Ethnography.

122. How long have you held that position?—Since 1896, having entered the Museum in 1880.

123. Will you give us any particulars you wish to add to what has been stated by Sir Edward Thompson as regards the acquisition of these Irish antiquities in the first place?—I do not think there is much for me to add with regard to that particular matter. The whole negotiation was a very simple matter, and it was done quite in the ordinary way of business, and I do not know that I have anything I should wish to add to the statement that Sir Edward Thompson has made which, of course, is practically my own statement.

124. I need hardly say you had no communications with any bodies in Ireland?—None whatever.

125. You did not give them any notice, and they did not call your attention to the matter?—No, I had no communication with them whatever.

126. Then, on the Irish aspect of the question, can you recall any instance where applications had been made to you by the Royal Irish Academy or any other body in Ireland with a view to their obtaining any object they desired to have without incurring the competition of the British Museum?—Of recent years, I think, since Colonel Plunkett has been at the Museum, we are very frequently corresponding, and he very frequently asks my advice about a good many things. No longer ago than yesterday morning I had a similar letter from him, but whether any request of precisely that character came I do not remember; I do not think so, in my time. On the other hand, my predecessor in office rendered very considerable benefits to the Royal Irish Academy by recommending, for instance, to the Government the purchase of the Petrie Collection. He was a friend of Sir William Wilde, who was the then Keeper of the Royal Irish Academy's Museum; he was on very intimate terms with, and knew the people, and it is not likely that anything would have come before him, except as a personal matter; as to that I cannot, of course, speak of my own knowledge.

127. It is the case, I think, that from time to time objects may be offered in the market in London without having been offered in Dublin or Edinburgh. Therefore, I suppose, the representative of the British Museum here would have opportunities of exercising those good offices you speak of, in the way of calling the attention of the Irish or Scottish Museums to objects which were in the market or coming into the market?—Unquestionably, on many occasions.

128. But you do not yourself recall any occasion since you have been at the Museum in which that has happened?—No, I think not with regard to Ireland. I should mention one thing that comes perhaps within that category. At the sale of the Fountaine Collection there was one very important object, which is beyond all question, I take it, of Irish interest; that is, the arm of Saint Lachtein; it was a reliquary which contained the arm of that Irish saint; it was called by his name. That was a very fine work of art, and had been in the English collection for more than a century. It was a collection made by Sir Andrew Fountaine. When the collection came to be sold at Christie's, my predecessor, Sir A. Wollaston Franks, wished to buy that reliquary; he was very keen about it indeed. He had some talk with Lord Powerscourt, who, I think, on that occasion more or less represented the Royal Irish Academy, and after discussing the matter, Sir Wollaston Franks gave way to Lord Powerscourt, and did not compete for that very fine work of art; one of the finest things, certainly, that has been sold in my time of this period of mediæval Irish art. That is now, I believe, in the Dublin Museum. It went for what seems now an absurdly low price, and it was not a very high one then.

129. Then, turning to Scotland, will you tell the Committee exactly what happened in the case of the purchase of the Glenlyon brooch?—There I think I can add something that is perhaps material. I do not think it seemed to be clear why, in the first place, in my negotiations with Mr Carfrae—whom, I may mention, I did recognise as the agent of the Scottish antiquaries—I offered to show him my report if he would first tell me what his limit was. My own experience tells me that whenever an agent is authorised to buy a particular thing at a sale by auction, he naturally has given him, by his principal, a limit beyond which he is not to go, or at least to a very trifling amount. My limit was practically fixed by my own Report, which had been written a week before and sent in to the Trustees, and was out of my hands. Therefore I thought if Mr Carfrae would say to me that he was going to 100*l.* for the brooch, for instance, my Report saying 300*l.*, I should then have advised him that he would lose it, according to my view. My desire was that it should be secured. If he had said he was going to 500*l.* or more, I should then have said, "Well, I will take the responsibility of retiring from the position." But Mr Carfrae gave me no such opening; he declined to say anything at all, and therefore my orders from the Trustees were to buy the brooch for 300*l.* or thereabouts—that is how I read them. Mr Carfrae does not give me any opening at all for making the slightest concession. The only thing he says is, "You must give it up to us," without assigning any reason except that it was a Scottish brooch, which I did not question. I hope I have made it clear why I took that particular course, and I do not think, in the position in which I then stood, I could have done anything else. There was barely time even to consult Sir Edward Thompson, because the sale was at one o'clock I think, and this conversation would be about eleven o'clock.

130. How long had it been within your knowledge that the Glenlyon brooch was coming to be offered for sale?—As a matter of fact it was offered to me by a jeweller, but he would not name a price, and I could not entertain it. Then the next I heard of it was at Christie's, which was probably a fortnight or three weeks before the day of the sale.

131. Was any communication made by you to the Scottish museums that this thing was likely to come into the market for sale?—No, none whatever. I regard my department as being a collection which should justify its name as the Department of British Antiquities; therefore I should not feel that I was called upon to advise anybody, in fact, beyond advising the Trustees that such a thing was coming up. It was my duty to secure it at a reasonable price. I take it that in this particular case my duty was very clear and simple.

132. But if a regulation or a rule had been in existence at that time, we will say promulgated by the Trustees of the British Museum for the sake of argument, that notice was to be given where the officers of the British Museum became aware that an article was coming into the market of special interest to Scotland or Ireland, there would have been no difficulty then in your informing the Society of Scottish Antiquaries as soon as you became aware of it yourself, then they would have had time to consider and act?—Just so.

133. As I understand your position it is that in the absence of any such rule or condition, you consider your first duty is to your own Museum, and that you should secure anything that you consider is of the nature of British interest for your own Museum?—Clearly.

134. Then if the Scottish or the Irish body interested happened to become aware of this they might, if time and opportunity served, interfere, and you would be disposed to enter into negotiations with them?—Decidedly. There never has been anything except on these two occasions otherwise than the most friendly relations. With regard to the most important Irish thing that had happened in my time, namely, with regard to the arm—the reliquary—there we gave way. With regard to another very important thing at Edinburgh, the part of one set of Chessmen, an arch of Chessmen from the Island of Lewis (this is a time ago that I am speaking of) there again Mr Anderson, who was the keeper of the Museum, wrote to Mr Wollaston Franks, and asked him not to compete. We have a very good series of these, and we judged that we could do without them, and out of friendly courtesy we did not compete for those things, and they are now, I think, in the Museum at Edinburgh.

135. There was one question which Sir Edward Thompson rather left for you, namely, what was the course of bidding in the case of the Glenlyon brooch? Of course at an auction it is very difficult to say who is really making the bids, because if a man is well known to be very likely to buy a thing of a particular class, the chances are that he will employ somebody else to do his bidding; but as far as I am aware Mr Carfrae had no agent at all; in fact the agent he would have employed naturally was the agent that I employ. I do not know. I have not heard from that day to this that he ever had an agent. He was standing beside my only agent being on my other side. I kept my eye upon him to see

Mr. C. H. Read, F.S.A. — 7 Dec 1898.

whether he was either bidding or going to bid, and I did not see him make any sign. Of course a very small sign is wanted in an auction room, but I saw him make no sign or move of any kind from the time that the bidding got beyond about 150*l*. It went very rapidly up to that sum, and then gradually slackened as the number of bidders lessened.

136. Who was the final bidder against you?—That is what I cannot say. I understood at the time that it was a private individual (one of the Carrises) but Mr Carrise has told me since that it was his bid; how he made it I do not know. He might have employed an agent, but I do not know that he did, nor has he told me that he did.

137. (*Sir T. Esmonde*) I notice in Sir Edward Thompson's statement the date of finding these Irish gold ornaments is given as the autumn of 1896?—No, it came to my notice then, but I think they were found in the spring.

138. If Sir Patrick Coll, of Dublin, states that these things were found in the month of January, 1897, evidently he is not very well informed?—I hope he is better informed about other things.

139. What is your opinion about these gold ornaments?—I have written my opinion of them. This is the briefest statement of the case that I can make, and although it contains some elementary statements I have tried to make it complete, even at that risk:—

"There is an idea prevalent that when Celtic art and Celtic civilisation are spoken of, the reference must of necessity be to Ireland or Scotland. This idea can only be held in ignorance of the facts. Up to the first establishment of the Roman power in England, there is no more reason for connecting the Celts with Ireland or Scotland, than with the South of England. During the Roman domination Celtic art considerably influenced that of their conquerors, but gradually disappeared in the parts of England nearest to the Continent, subsisting only in the less accessible parts of Britain and Ireland. There it remained as a living art during the pagan times of Britain, and it is to this seclusion that we owe its existence in early mediaeval times.

"But, during the earlier period to which the objects now in question belong, which may be roughly called from 300 B.C. to 100 A.D., the Celtic population who created this remarkable form of art was spread not only over the whole of the South of England, but was widely distributed over the Continent. In Germany, Austria, France, Switzerland, Italy, and even further afield, remains of this artistic race are found, differing only in time and relatively in style.

"But it was in Britain about the beginning of our era, that the art attained its highest development, and this country stands without a rival for the quality of its late Celtic work.

"My predecessor in office, the late Sir A. Wollaston Franks, was the first to separate the antiquities of this class into a category of their own under the name of Late Celtic, a term which has been generally adopted in England. Before the publication of the work edited by him and called 'Horae Ferales,' they had been a puzzle to antiquaries, some calling them Roman while others assigned them to a later period.

"During the whole time that he was in the British Museum Sir Wollaston Franks never missed an opportunity of securing any remains belonging to this period, and the result is a fine series, worthy of his knowledge and pertinacity. In preparing the volume of "Horae Ferales," which I may mention is the standard work on the subject, he necessarily gathered together the best existing examples of the peculiar form of art which he had made the subject of study. I have made an analysis of the various localities in which the specimens illustrated and mentioned were found, with the following results, viz.:

"From Switzerland 17 objects, from France seven, Germany 13, Scotland nine, Ireland eight, and from England 56.

"It will scarcely be asserted by anyone who knew Sir Wollaston Franks and his methods, that he would allow any bias to interfere with his archaeological work. He would naturally select the best and most characteristic examples that he could find. He was well acquainted with both the Scottish and Irish collections, and was in fact an intimate friend of Sir William Wilde, then keeper of the Irish collections. It is, therefore, not unfair to assume that he found the best and most characteristic specimens among those from English discoveries. The form of art known as Late Celtic is, therefore, pre-eminently English.

"The bare fact that an object, particularly if made of precious metal, is found in a locality is by no means evidence that it necessarily has any other connection with the place. In the present case the circumstances seem rather to lead to an opposite conclusion, viz., that these golden objects were the prey of some piratical foray, and therefore in all probability belonged elsewhere than where they were found. Instances are not wanting in support of this contention with regard to Ireland. A hoard of silver objects, comprising fragments of Roman plate so hacked and cut up as to show conclusively that there was no value attached to them except as metal, was found at Coleraine in the year 1831, with these were found small coins denarii, &c., of Roman emperors from Constantine II.

"In the account of this find published in the Proceedings of the Royal Irish Academy (vol. ii., p. 182), Dr. Drummond, endeavouring to show how the objects came there, says:—'There is yet another mode of accounting for these remains of antiquity, not less plausible. The early Irish, like the neighbouring nations, were fond of making predatory excursions. They often landed on the shores of England and Wales, and carried off whatever spoil fell into their hands. Of the spoils by which they were sometimes enriched it may suffice to mention an instance, extracted from O'Flaherty's Ogygia, ii., pp. 182-83. Crimthan Niadnar, the 111th monarch of Ireland, towards the end of the first century, returned from a 'foreign expedition in which he obtained a very rich booty, among which was a golden chariot, a pair of tables studded with 300 brilliant gems, a quilt of various colours, a cloak interwoven with threads of gold, a sword engraved with various figures of serpents, which were of the purest gold, a shield embossed with refulgent silver studs, a spear which always gave an incurable wound; a sling so unerring that it never missed; two hounds coupled with a chain which, being made of silver, was worth 300 cows, with other valuable rarities.'"

"The same author informs us that, about the middle of the third century, Cormac, the Irish monarch of Ireland 'equipped a large fleet which he sent to the north of Britain where he was committing depredations for three years' (p. 330).

"The great diversity of style, as well as the difference in the quality of the gold of the various objects comprised in the hoard, points very clearly to some such explanation as the foregoing of their being found together. Further, there is nothing in the character of the work that is especially Irish. On the contrary, the closest analogy for the most particular feature, viz., the gold chains, is seen in an English discovery of the same period, two bracelets from Lancashire, and Mr. A. J. Evans, in his paper on the discovery, finds the nearest analogue to the highly ornamental gold collar in a shield from the Thames. Nor even if it be granted that the boat is a model of a curragh—this form of boat was fully as English as it was at a later period Irish.

"I do not consider that there is any proof, archaeological or otherwise, that this hoard has any but an accidental connection with Ireland. The probability is fully as great, if not greater, that these objects were the production of the people popularly known as the Ancient Britons. As such they are most interesting illustrations of British history, and could nowhere be more appropriately placed than in the British Museum, the central museum of the empire." That gives you in brief my view of the relations of these objects to the British Museum primarily and by implication elsewhere.

140. (*Chairman*) They were for a good many hundreds of years, at all events, entombed in Ireland?—Yes, it is very probable.

141. (*Sir T. Esmonde*) This is a very interesting paper, but is it a question rather for antiquarians?—It is an antiquarian matter, no doubt.

142. I am very glad to have your opinion about these gold ornaments, but I want to ask you not so much as to their character, but as to their value from an archaeological point of view?—That is practically answered by my report to the Trustees, that I considered their value to be 600*l*.

143. But from the antiquarian point of view what do you think their value is?—I must refer you to the report. There are two kinds of value to an object, one is the amount of money that you can get for it in the market, and the other is the historical or archaeological or antiquarian interest; in the one case the value is 600*l*., in the other you have my opinion in the report which I sent to the Trustees, which Sir Edward Thompson has read, and my general view of the matter is given in the paper that I have read to you at this moment. I do not know what other point of view there can be.

Mr. C. H. Read, F.S.A.

1 Dec. 1898.

143. You are certain they are Celtic work?—There is no question of that. They belonged to the class that has been universally accepted—I think I may say universally—as what is called late Celtic Art. That is to say, they belong to a period when iron was used, and so on.

144. We had an expression of opinion, I think, that they might be Roman?—

145. (*Sir John Evans.*) What do you consider the dates are?—It is rather difficult to discriminate as to precisely what is Roman and what is Celtic, seeing that these people were working at the same time, and, as I stated, they influenced the art of the Romans. This particular form of chase is certainly an Oriental style, and might, therefore, have come with the Celts in the early times from the north east or wherever they came from.

146. (*Sir T. Esmonde.*) In the British Museum you have a very fine collection of Celtic gold ornaments?—Not of Celtic gold ornaments. We have a good collection, but not of gold ornaments. They are bronze chiefly.

147. You have not, for instance, such a good collection of gold ornaments as they have in Dublin?—I think not, although it is more than a quarter of a century since I have seen the Dublin collection.

148. There was some paper read at one of the societies I think on the subject?—A paper was read by Mr. A. J. Evans, which I referred to in my report. That was read at the Society of Antiquaries on the 14th January last year.

149. There is no statement made there as to the exact place at which these things were found?—No.

150. It was not generally known then, I presume?—I did not know it, and Mr. Evans could not know it as far as I am aware. It was certainly not generally known.

151. Have you any idea if the Royal Irish Academy knew anything about it at that time?—I should think they ought to have done. At that time they had been found about a year. If it had been my business I think I should have heard of it before a twelvemonth had passed, but I had no communication from them, and therefore I cannot say. Of my own knowledge I know nothing whatever as to what they knew in the matter.

152. And you have no idea as to whether the Royal Irish Academy had any opportunity of offering for these gold ornaments. They were never offered to them, were they?—No, nor were they offered to me as far as I know.

153. (*Chairman.*) When you say they were not offered are you speaking of these gold ornaments?—Yes, they were not offered to me, I asked for them. The owner did not bring them to England for the purpose of selling them, as far as I know. One cannot tell, of course, what a man's motives are, and I do not go into that at all. Mr. Day brings them here, and they appear to me to be things which would be rightly placed in the British Museum; then I approach Mr. Day and say, "If you think of selling them at any time I think they ought to go to the British Museum." Mr. Day says, probably, that he had not thought of it, or something like that. I cannot recollect exactly what he did say, but if he did he would give me the refusal, and then negotiations went on.

154. (*Sir T. Esmonde.*) Did Mr. Day say he would give you the refusal of them?—Probably he would put me off at first. I do not say he used those particular words, but that would be the impression created in my mind—that if he would sell them to anybody he would probably let me know.

155. Then you had no idea that he was in communication with anybody else for the purpose of selling them?—No.

156. He said nothing about being in communication with the Royal Irish Academy?—No, nothing at all.

157. So that as far as you are aware the Royal Irish Academy had not been communicated with in the matter up to this time?—Of course that I do not know.

158. You did not know that they were anyhow?—No.

159. So that of course you acted in this matter without any idea of walking on the corns of the Royal Irish Academy?—We had no idea of the kind.

160. They had not been communicated with so far as you are aware, and you thought that you had a free hand?—Certainly. I considered it my duty, as I do in the case of the Glastonbury brooch or any other important object which comes within my cognisance—if it is a suitable thing for the British Museum and I have the money to buy it, I consider that my first duty is to recommend the Trustees to buy it.

161. If I were in your position I should probably think the same?—I do not think there can be any question about it.

162. Have you any idea what is the position of the Royal Irish Academy with regard to these objects; not as regards these particular objects, but Irish antiquities generally?—Are you asking me as to the importance of their position?

163. No. What is the official position with regard to Irish antiquities generally—we will say gold ornaments, to make it more precise?—I should take it that their position is much the same as that of the British Museum with regard to British antiquities, is it not?

164. I do not pretend to know what the position of the British Museum is with regard to British antiquities.—If important things in these classes come forward in the market or in private possession, or what not, it is the duty of the respective heads of departments to try and secure such as are suited for the collection. That is the position that they would take up.

165. The British Museum has no better standing than that in regard to these things?—We have no preemptive right to any antiquities at all that I know of. Most British antiquities, I am sorry to say, are purchased.

166. Have you any preemptive right to purchase?—No.

167. What is the position with regard to English treasure trove?—It goes to the Treasury.

168. And from there?—I am not in a position to go into the very complicated law of treasure trove, but what happens usually is this. Suppose a find of coins is found, the finder gives notice, or is made to give notice, to the police or magistrate that he has made a discovery in the nature of treasure trove, and he goes to the Treasury. The Treasury then—and this has happened several times in my time—sends these objects to the British Museum, and asks us to be good enough to furnish them with a report of the bullion or intrinsic value and the market value; or, in the case of objects which some value was less, the archaeological value of the objects, and at the same time to state whether we want any of them. We do this, and the things go back—or in any case they went to the South Kensington Museum. That find of silver plate on Parliament Hill was referred to me, and as it seemed a better find for the South Kensington Museum than the British Museum—being rather modern—they have gone to the South Kensington Museum.

169. Then in the case of English treasure trove the Treasury communicates with the British Museum authorities when the treasure is found?—That is the usual course, yes.

170. (*Mr. John Morley.*) Is it handed as a free gift either to you or South Kensington?—Oh, no, we have to pay for it.

171. (*Sir T. Esmonde.*) That is your position as far as treasure trove in England is concerned, but you are not aware what is the position of the Royal Irish Academy so far as Irish treasure trove is concerned?—I cannot say that I know. In fact, the position of the British Museum is exceedingly ill-defined, and the whole law of treasure trove seems to me a hopeless muddle.

172. You are aware that the position of the Royal Irish Academy towards treasure trove in Ireland is more or less the same as that of the British Museum towards treasure trove in England?—I do not know anything about it, but I can quite imagine that it is.

173. You have never been aware of that circumstance, and you are not aware of that now?—No.

174. Now, with regard to these gold ornaments, has there been any communication between the Royal Irish Academy and the British Museum?—With regard to this matter?

175. Yes, since their purchase?—That, I think, Sir Edward Thompson ought to have answered, because nothing went through me. Officially, of course, all communications to the British Museum from the Royal Irish Academy, or any other body, should come to the head of the museum, and then he would refer it to the official concerned. That would be the strictly official course, but of course I need not say that official life would be impossible if everything went through that

Mr. C. H. Read, F.S.A.

7 Dec. 1898.

painful process, therefore Col. Plunkett writes direct to me about certain things with which he knows that I am concerned, instead of writing to Sir Edward Thompson and the latter sending the communication on to me, but nothing has come so far as I know.

176. Either before or after the sale?—After the sale.

177. (*Sir Edward Thompson.*) The first communication came up through the Treasury.

(*Witness.*) Sir Edward Thompson might have asked me to look at these statements and see whether they were accurate or not, but the letter came from the Treasury to him, therefore technically it is not from the Royal Irish Academy.

178. It was Mr. Robert Day that the trustees purchased from?—Yes.

179. You have already said that you did not know whether Mr. Day had had any communication with the Royal Irish Academy before the purchase?—No, I could not know anything about that.

180. Mr. Day sold the gold ornaments, and of course he is quite satisfied with having done so, but has he made any communication to you or the British Museum, or to any other official department with reference to these gold ornaments?—Yes.

181. Do you know what it was?—That again Sir Edward Thompson should know. I think on one or two occasions he wrote, offering to buy them back again. I am not cognisant of the whole of the matter.

(*Sir Edward Thompson.*) The matter came up to us through the Treasury. An application was made to the Treasury from the Royal Irish Academy. The Royal Irish Academy wrote to the Under Secretary at Dublin, the Under Secretary wrote to the Treasury, and the Treasury sent it on to us.

(*Chairman.*) What is the date of that?—

Sir Edward Thompson.—The letter from the Royal Irish Academy is 19th April 1898, the letter from the Under Secretary is 27th April 1898, and the Treasury letter to us is 30th April 1898. Then it came before the Trustees.

(*Chairman.*) Was that before or after the purchase?—

(*Sir John Evans.*) A year after the purchase and a year and a quarter after they were exhibited.

(*Witness.*) I, of course, only heard the result of these letters. From whom the suggestion came could not matter to me.

(*Sir T. Esmonde.*) Mr. Day has offered to purchase them back, has he?

(*Sir E. Thompson.*) He made an offer and then withdrew it.

(*Chairman.*) I will read to you the actual letter: "Myrtle Hill House, Cork, April 18th, 1898. Sir,—During the past year the trustees of the British Museum purchased from me for 600*l.* some Celtic gold ornaments that were found in the North of Ireland. I believe it is your wish that I should write and inform you that I will repay the trustees the above-named amount if they will transfer the ornaments to me, and that upon their doing so I will hand them over to the Royal Irish Academy, who in their turn will reimburse me for them. I have, &c., ROBERT DAY." Then there is this note at the side, "This offer was, I understand, subsequently withdrawn."

(*Sir E. Thompson.*) Mr. Day withdrew the offer on the 19th May. I have the letter here. Mr. Day's offer to repurchase was passed on to me, and I got into correspondence with him, explaining the position of things. He wrote on the 19th May, 1898: "Dear Sir,—In answer to your letter referring to the Celtic gold ornaments, which I am sorry had not an earlier reply, I beg to withdraw my offer to the Chancellor of the Exchequer, and hope the objects will have their permanent home in the British Museum."

(*Chairman.*) I understand that the offer had been made to the Chancellor of the Exchequer and Trustees of the British Museum, not *qua* Chancellor of the Exchequer?

(*Sir Edward Thompson.*) I do not know exactly why Mr. Day went to the Chancellor of the Exchequer. I suppose dealing with money matters Mr. Day thought the proper quarter to write to was the Exchequer.

182-3. (*Sir T. Esmonde.*) The Royal Irish Academy, so far as you are aware, made no effort whatever to get hold of these gold ornaments before they were offered to the British Museum?—None.

184. Therefore, in your opinion, the responsibility for losing these gold ornaments rests with them?—Unquestionably it seems so to me.

185. (*Sir Herbert Maxwell.*) I understand that the only case in which you have had any sort of disagreement with the Society of Scottish Antiquaries is the case of the Glenlyon brooch?—Yes, that is the only thing that has come within my knowledge.

186. And you say that might easily have been avoided by better arrangements on their part?—I think so, if you like to put it in that way. I think a little common sense on the part of the agent might have made the thing very simple.

187. Naturally you do not wish to find yourself in competition with the Scottish National Museum?—It is most unpleasant, and in most cases most unlikely, I think.

188. As the accident has happened, do you agree with Sir Edward Thompson that it would be very undesirable to give discretionary power to the Trustees to rectify not in an individual case, or in one or two cases, but to give them a general power of setting miscarriages of that nature right?—My answer all depends upon the definition of the word "miscarriage."

189. I use it in the sense of an historical national object leaving the Kingdom whence it derives its particular interest?—It has not left the kingdom in this case. I mean it still remains in the kingdom.

(*Mr. John Morley.*) And it is in "the United Kingdom" also.

190. (*Sir Herbert Maxwell.*) If that is going on the notes I should like to ask this. The historical interest of the Glenlyon brooch arose long before the Union of Scotland with England?—That is possible.

191. Is it not the case that any historical interest which it possesses arose long before the Union?—Yes, certainly.

192. Then if, I will not call it a miscarriage, but if a circumstance occurs which conveys out of the kingdom which confers the historic interest any object into another kingdom, do you object to any power being given to your Trustees to gratify the natural desire of the people of either country?—I should think it would be most difficult to confer such a power without imposing a most undesirable amount of responsibility upon the Trustees. I should be sorry for the Trustees if the responsibility were put upon them of having to decide between the rival claims in such cases as you put. I think the Trustees would rather avoid it, and I certainly think it would lead to more trouble than profit to anyone.

193-201. Then you would disregard the national feeling altogether?—I do not know anything about national feeling; I am a keeper of British antiquities.

202. (*Sir John Evans.*) If a mistake occurs it can be rectified, can it not, before the article is entered on the register?—Before the bill is paid.

203. There is always power to do that?—Yes.

204. And there was no attempt to get anything rectified in the case of this brooch?—No, no attempt was made, I believe.

205. If the British Museum purchases an object, and finds that in purchasing it it has made some mistake, any mistake of that kind can be rectified before the bill is passed for payment, and before the object is inscribed in the register of the museum?—I believe that is the case.

206. And there is no suggestion that there was such a mistake in the case of this brooch?—No, except Mr. Carfrae's statement that I ought not to buy it, which perhaps implied that.

207. But there was no effort made to rectify the mistake?—No, I believe not.

208. If you had been aware that Mr. Carfrae was empowered to bid 200*l.*, if he had told you that, you would not have bidden against him?—I should not. I should have thought that the preponderating interest was on his side.

209. With regard to communicating with Scottish or Irish museums in the case of a Scottish or Irish object being sold in London, do you consider it the business of the British Museum to inform them of that, or their business to inform the British Museum and ask them not to compete?—I should think the latter, that they should ask us if we are going to bid. If we could meet them we should, but they should apply to us, not we to them.

610. Are you aware of the length of time that elapsed between the exhibition in London of the objects of late Celtic art and the application from the Royal Irish Academy, with regard to them?—I cannot of my own knowledge say that.

611. The exhibition was on the 14th January, and the first application from the Royal Irish Academy was in February 1898, so that they apparently did not take much interest in the matter?—The first record I have is the 14th May.

612. Mr. Day is a member of the Royal Irish Academy?—Yes.

613. You do not know whether he communicated as to these objects with them?—I do not.

614. Where is the best collection of late Celtic antiquities, if you had to study late Celtic antiquities, what museum would you go to?—I should say the British Museum.

615. It is far superior in respect of late Celtic art to any other museum in the world?—I should think so.

616. I believe that late Celtic art was a speciality of the Wollaston Franks?—It was.

617. And that he not only purchased, on account of the museum, but that he gave a large number of objects himself?—That is so.

618. And he induced others who happened to have late Celtic antiquities to present them to the museum? —Yes, he went as far as that.

619. Do you see that there is any Irish interest attaching to these gold ornaments beyond the fact that they were found in Ireland?—I do not see that there is necessarily anything. It may be claimed that some part of them are Irish work, but there is fully as much evidence, as I have shown in my note, that they are English.

620. And their presence in the British Museum rather fills a gap, I believe?—It does, most distinctly. Almost every piece of the gold find is a novelty; it was not before represented in the collection.

621. And how would it be in Ireland?—I do not know. It could not fail to be of considerable interest in any museum, because it is a very exceptional discovery.

622. Can you tell me in what part of Europe the nearest analogue to the hollow collar was found?—I do not remember.

623. Was not there one found in Belgium?—Yes; I forget the name of the place now.

624. How is the collection in Dublin of late Celtic objects as compared with the British Museum?—It is so long since I have been there that I am not really able to answer that.

625. (*Chairman.*) You say that if Mr. Curle had told you that he was prepared to go to 200*l.* for that (Hunterston) brooch, you would have let him have it, as you consider that it had a preponderating interest for Scotland?—Other things being equal, certainly he had the preponderating interest.

626. And, therefore, that was a case at all events in which, supposing the regulation were in existence authorising you, where any article came into the market which had a special interest for either Scotland or Ireland—in this instance for Scotland—from the place of its finding or some other circumstance—supposing, I say, there had been a regulation that you should in such circumstances communicate with the national museum, this would have been a case in which you would have informed them of the fact that such an article was coming for sale?—Before buying it, if there was such a regulation, I should consider it my duty to ask whether they would compete with us.

627. I do not understand you to say that such a regulation as that would lead to any unpleasant consequences?—None at all, except that there is no such regulation, the practice is precisely what you described.

628. But what I mean is this: there was one of your answers which gave me rather a different impression; you seemed to say that the establishment of such regulations would lead to a greater amount of friction than exists at present?—It was on another point entirely that I made that answer to Sir Herbert Maxwell; with regard to giving powers to the Trustees to part with what they had already purchased. That is quite a different point.

629. I am glad that I have cleared up that. Would you see any objection to regulations authorising you not only to communicate with the institution of the country which might have a preponderating interest in some article that came for sale, but also authorising you not to interfere by bidding against the representative of that country for such an article. Would you see any objection to such a rule?—Generally speaking, there would be no objection to such a rule as that, but, of course, it would have to be observed in a reasonable way by both sides.

630. In a catholic spirit?—In a catholic spirit.

631. (*Sir Herbert Maxwell.*) I think you said if representations had been made on the part of the Society of Scottish Antiquaries in time, the mistake, assuming it to be a mistake or misunderstanding, might have been rectified?—Yes.

632. The sale was on the 21st May?—Yes.

633. And the Scottish Antiquaries wrote to the Trustees on the 29th May?—Yes, but that was eight days too late. When you buy a thing by auction you have bought it the moment the hammer falls.

634. What do I understand the nature of the representation ought to have been?—What I said rather referred not to a sale by auction, because, as I say, you cannot recall the matter once it is completed. If I instruct an agent to buy for the British Museum at an auction sale, the moment the hammer falls the British Museum has bought that object, and cannot go back, and the agent is entitled to his commission as well. I mean there are two persons you have to deal with, and you cannot go back upon those things.

635. (*Sir T. Esmonde.*) You would limit your answer to any question to the case of purchases of private persons?—Undoubtedly, it could not be otherwise.

636. (*Sir Herbert Maxwell.*) The only point I had in my mind was this, that there was no possibility of representations being made on the part of the Scottish Antiquaries?—I do not wish to say that that is not quite accurate, but except that we both employed the same agent, as would have done, there is no reason why the agent should not have known at least 24 hours before.

637. But when it was once knocked down to you?—In those cases any representation must necessarily be made before the sale. After the sale neither the buyer, nor the auctioneer generally, will hear anything about rectifying the purchase.

638. (*Sir T. Esmonde.*) I think you said you had no idea of any sort that the Royal Irish Academy wanted to get hold of these ornaments or to enter into negotiations about them?—What I said was that I had not heard that they had taken any steps towards obtaining them.

639. And you had no reason to suppose that they wanted to get them?—None at all, except that they were very fine things. I had no special reason beyond the general ground that anybody would like to possess antiquities of this kind. I had no ground for thinking that the Royal Irish Academy would be dissatisfied with any action that I took, if it resulted in the articles becoming the property of the British Museum. I think that is clear.

SECOND DAY.

Tuesday, 13th December 1898.

PRESENT

The Right Hon. The Lord RATHMORE (*Chairman*).

Sir T. GRATTAN ESMONDE, Bart., M.P.	The Right Hon. Sir HERBERT E. MAXWELL, Bart., M.P.
The Right Hon. Sir JOHN LUBBOCK, Bart., M.P.	The Right Hon. JOHN MORLEY, M.P.

L. J. HEWBY, Esq., *Secretary*.

Prof. ROBERT ATKINSON, LL.D., called; and Examined.

940. (*Chairman.*) I believe you are secretary to the council of the Royal Irish Academy?—Yes.

941. How long have you been secretary?—Twenty years.

942. I daresay you have seen the terms of reference made to this Committee?—Yes.

943. I will ask you on the first head of that reference—that is to say, as to the circumstances under which certain Celtic ornaments were recently offered for sale to the British Museum—to tell us what the Council of the Royal Irish Academy wish to present to this Committee on that subject?—We had no knowledge of anything of the kind being possible until it was announced in the *Athenæum* newspaper. On the appearance of the résumé of the paper that was read by Mr. Evans, I laid it before the Council. I had up to that time no knowledge whatever of anything of the kind having been found, but the moment I saw it, it was obvious to me, at least, it was *primâ facie* in the category of treasure trove. The Council appointed a committee to inquire into the circumstances so far as they might, because they, too, felt the same thing. The committee authorised practically my going to the Crown Solicitor to ask for further details about the matter, because in the résumé that appeared in the paper there was nothing said as to the finder, and it was thought that as we, the Council, had no machinery to find out the real finder, the proper thing was to move the Crown Solicitor and have the authorities take such steps as they deemed right to ascertain his name and the place of the find. I accordingly went to the Crown Solicitor, but Sir Patrick Coll told me that he had no information, and could give me none, and that he could not move the constabulary in an until I could furnish definite information as to the place and time and person. Now, my lord, we had had occasion to move in matters of treasure trove. We had been directed by the constabulary to inform certain persons who had said treasure trove objects, or what *primâ facie* were so, that that was not the proper procedure. Therefore I had written to persons to inform them, and that, too, on the direction of the constabulary or of the authorities, that their procedure was not right, and that they should transmit the objects to the Academy. The Academy has had, all the time of my secretaryship, that duty distinctly imposed upon it, and it has been enforced upon them practically by the conditions that have always been laid upon them that they should, when the constabulary moved them, send down a letter and request that the objects that thus appeared to be treasure trove should be forwarded to the Academy. Till 1860 or 1861 payments for treasure trove were made through the constabulary. Till 1862 there was a sum of £100 given to us to expend in respect of treasure trove, and that we disposed of in this way. Consequently, it was quite in keeping with that general regulation that I should move the Crown Solicitor, but as I have said, Sir Patrick Coll told me that nothing could be done. I had to go back *re infectâ*, because he said he could not move except upon definite information as to place, time, and person. I went to my committee and told them that, saying, "We must wait till Parliament meets, when there will be a chance of finding out who the finder is." When Parliament met a question was asked in the House of Commons, and the answer transpired.

944. (*Sir T. G. Esmonde.*) What date was that?—It was the 28th March, 1898.

945. (*Chairman.*) That was after the purchase by the British Museum?—Yes, the purchase had of course been made in the interim. We could not move, as I said, until Parliament met. When Parliament met this question was put, and the answer of the Attorney-General was quite categorical. I have a copy of Hansard here. The question put to the Attorney-General was "Whether the Celtic ornaments discovered recently in Donegal were treasure trove; if so, was an offence committed in handing them over to the agents of the British Museum, and will the Executive call for a report on this matter, or take any steps to prevent ancient remains passing out of Ireland in future?" Mr. Atkinson replied: "On the facts, so far as I have been able to ascertain them, these articles were, in my opinion, treasure trove, and belonged to the Crown. The first finder was *primâ facie* guilty of the offence of unlawfully, wilfully, and knowingly concealing the finding from the Crown. The ornaments were purchased by the trustees of the British Museum in the usual way of business from a private person, who, it is understood, had obtained them from a dealer. The first finder was, I am informed, a man named Thomas Nicholl, a farm servant in the employment of a Mr. Gibson, who lives near Limavady. I have not as yet been able to ascertain the number of intermediaries through whose hands the ornaments passed before their acquisition by the British Museum. The police have already all necessary directions as to their duties to prevent treasure trove from being improperly disposed of by persons who may find it." Then the report goes on:—"(Mr. W. H. K. Redmond): May I ask the right hon. gentleman the Secretary to the Treasury if, in view of the statement just made, he cannot make representations to the British Museum authorities with a view to having these ornaments returned to Ireland? (Mr. Hanbury): I do not think the Trustees of the British Museum have power to let them out of their custody unless it were proved that they had acquired them illegally. (Mr. P. O'Brien): Will any proceedings be taken against the finder of these articles, so as to make better known the state of the law? (Mr. Atkinson): On the information in my possession at present I cannot answer that question. (Mr. Clancy): Will the right hon. gentleman consider the propriety of prosecuting the Trustees of the British Museum? (Mr. Atkinson): No, sir."

946. You had heard that certain articles which were presumably treasure trove had been found. Not then, I say that they were likely to be disposed of to the British Museum or to anybody else, you were proceeding on the ground of your claim to these articles as treasure trove?—Precisely, as having been definitely treasure trove.

947. Are you now going back to the circumstances of the purchase by the British Museum? If you are not going back to it I should like to ask you this question: Whether you received any notice which would lead you to suppose that these articles were likely to be purchased by the British Museum or anyone else?—No notice whatever. I had not the slightest conception even that any such procedure would be attempted. It seemed to me so clear that *primâ facie* the objects were treasure trove, and that of necessity as soon as we found out who the finder was they must come to the Academy for valuation and consequent deposit in the Museum, that any alternative never occurred to me, and, as a matter of fact, I never heard a single syllable about it till I was told that the objects had been purchased by the British Museum. I never heard the question mooted as to whether they were tre-

[illegible] trove or not. That I could not conceive, because they seemed presumptively so positively treasure trove objects, and they were so thoroughly in keeping with the kind of objects and the kind of find that we regularly have to deal with, that it seemed to me that they would necessarily and inevitably come to the Academy in the ordinary way.

248. Then pursuing the line of examination that I was on just now, it was stated to us by Sir Edward Thompson that the Trustees of the British Museum sanctioned the purchase at a meeting of the Standing Committee on the 9th April, 1897; the order for payment was issued on the 13th May—I presume 1897. But it appears that you did not move in Parliament until the early part of 1898. I want to ask you when was it that you became aware that the British Museum had purchased these articles. It was stated here that the purchase was completed on the 13th May, 1897?—So far as my recollection goes I have nothing whatever about the purchase until after the Parliament had come.

249. That is 1897?—1897.

250. (Sir Herbert Maxwell.) Was it brought to your notice first by the article in the *Athenæum*?—Yes, absolutely.

251. (Sir John Lubbock.) That was in January, 1897?—Yes.

252. (Chairman.) What Dr. Atkinson says is that, when he first heard of the finding of these articles, he and the [illegible] of the Academy, was entirely directed to the recovery of them as treasure trove in the ordinary course, and that he was not aware that they had been actually purchased by the British Museum until after the Parliament of 1897.

(Sir John Lubbock.) And no steps were taken to recover them till March, 1898.

253. (Chairman.) Now, Dr. Atkinson, will you proceed?—I have here a synopsis of all the dates. January 28th was the meeting of the Society of Antiquaries, when Mr Evans's paper was read. On February 1st, 1897, the attention of the Council was called to the matter.

254. (Sir John Lubbock.) Are you correct about that, because we are told that the meeting was held on the 14th January, and that the report of it appeared on the 30th January?—Perhaps that is so.

255. (Chairman.) At any rate, the first you heard of it was the report of the 30th January?—Yes. On the 15th February there was another Committee meeting called to draw the attention of the Council to the fact, and there was a resolution passed that it was desirable to call the attention of the Irish Government to the breach of arrangement, by which treasure trove found in Ireland was placed in the Royal Irish Academy Museum. There nothing appeared possible for us to do, save the preparation of the memorial.* On the 21st February the Committee were instructed to prepare a memorial and forward the same to the Lord-Lieutenant. On the 7th March the memorial was forwarded, and we received in reply a letter from the Lord-Lieutenant, asking for further details.

256. Is that still 1897?—No, this is 1898. From February, 1897, to February, 1898, we had absolutely no opportunity of doing anything whatever, because we did not know what was done with the objects, and we did not know at all what steps the Government were taking to secure the name of the finder; during that interval we had no details of what was going on. I believe no hint came to us at all of what was going on during that period.

257. That is to say, you had no knowledge that the British Museum had purchased these articles, and that they were in their custody?—No, we knew nothing about it. However, we forwarded the memorial. The Lord-Lieutenant requested more precise particulars, and then we sent him on March 22nd. It was on the 25th March that a report appeared in the newspapers of particulars given by the Attorney-General for Ireland in the House of Commons, and then it was for the first time that we knew who the finder really was. Until that answer was given which we saw in the newspapers, we had no knowledge whatever of any definite kind that could have enabled us to move in our normal way. The normal way was clearly by an appeal to the Lord-Lieutenant. I think there was a sort of feeling that it was better that we should act through the Irish Government rather than have any communication with outside parties.

258. You were relying on the view that the objects were treasure trove objects, which would come to you according to the law?—That was the definite view—that these were proved *facie* treasure trove, and that they must come to us. It could not have entered the head of anybody that they would be claimed as saleable in the open market. I would have scouted the idea if anybody had told me that these were to be sold in the open market. Although the circumstances were not definitely set down as I think they should have been in Mr Evans's paper, there was quite enough in that paper to show that these objects were, in fact, treasure trove. They were the very best ideal of a treasure trove, and, therefore, it could not be supposed for a moment that they would be offered for sale in the open market.

Prof. Atkinson, LL.D.

13 Dec. 1898.

259. (Sir John Lubbock.) Who has ever said anything about the open market?—I was not aware that there was any question of open market in the matter, if you mean by that an ordinary sale?—As I have just read to you what the Attorney-General in Parliament said was, "The ornaments were purchased by the Trustees of the British Museum in the usual way of business." I do not know precisely what that means, but I infer that it was not as a treasure trove purchase. The Attorney-General says—"They were purchased from a private person, who, it is understood, had obtained them from a dealer." Now, the one point that we have found upon us, is that we have nothing to do with intermediaries; no dealer can intervene in the matter of treasure trove. If any dealer had brought any of these objects to me, and asked me to purchase them for the Academy, whatever their value or interest may have been, I should have declined, because we only deal with the finder. The Treasury minute of 1861 directs us to deal with the finder, and not with any dealer. No intermediary is allowed to intervene. The finder was to bring the articles to us, or to the Constabulary; we were to name the price, and the finder was to accept that, so that there could not be any question of purchase or sale in the matter.

260. (Chairman.) Could you fix approximately the date at which you became aware that these objects had been purchased by the British Museum?—I do not think I knew anything about it until the beginning of this year.

261. Was it at the instance of the Irish Academy, or any members of it, so far as you know, that action was taken in the House of Commons about it?—I do not know how that was done. I have confined myself entirely to my functions as Secretary of the Council.

262. You considered that your official business was to look after the treasure trove in the ordinary way by applying to the Irish Government?—Yes, because I have been doing it for twenty years, and I have been directed time after time to do it. Indeed, I had also done it with reference to Mr Day, who interfered, rightly or wrongly, in this matter. I had been directed two years before by the Constabulary, that is, Dublin Castle, to write to Mr Day, and inform him that certain objects which he had purchased in Cork were treasure trove, and should be sent to us. He sent me a letter on that occasion, declining to do so, and stating the treasure trove law as he had expounded it. He thought better of it when he had read the details of the treasure trove law, and on the 25th April, 1898, he sent us the articles.

263. Do you say 1898?—Yes, that was the date of the previous occasion. When I speak of it, that I had informed Mr Day precisely what our position was in regard to treasure trove.

264. Do you mean as regards this particular find?—No. That was on a former occasion. I mention that to show that I had done this as portion of my duty as Secretary of the Council. When the reports in the newspapers appeared with the Attorney-General's answer, in which he stated that in his opinion these articles were treasure trove, I felt perfectly satisfied, because, I said, if the Government have received the opinion of their authoritative legal officer that these things are treasure trove, the question must be treated; and in that I expected to see it. What happened was this. There was a discussion about it, but very shortly after we received a letter from Mr Day, enclosing copy of a letter he had addressed to the Chancellor of the Exchequer, offering to refund the money to the British Museum, and saying that he would transfer the objects to us, and that we should pay him £600. Now, when that proposal came up, I felt very strongly that £600 was nearly a fancy price. We have been in the habit in purchasing these gold ornaments of giving, say, twice or thrice the bullion value of them, but we have never given such an extravagant price as that. I think, taking the weight of these objects, £70 or £80 would be about the bullion value, so that I think we might have

* See Appendix III.

Prof. R. Atkinson, LL.D.

15 Dec 1898.

given £300 or £350; but such a figure as £300 seemed to be rather a competition price, which I am sure the Council of the Academy would not, at any rate upon my initiative, have offered.

265. I understand you to say that in no case would you have purchased these particular things which you consider ought to come to you as treasure trove?—That is the real point.

266. But if that reason had not applied, you would have considered £300 an ample price to pay for them?—I am speaking, of course, only personally. That would be the price if they had come to us in the ordinary way through the Constabulary. I have here a notice to finders. It shows the very formal way in which the thing is done:—

"To Finders of Antiquities in Ireland.—The Royal Irish Academy has for many years past endeavoured to preserve for the nation every procurable article illustrative of the ancient history and people of Ireland. Irish antiquities offered for sale to the Academy are valued [illegible] by a committee, who decide the prices to be given for them, which are higher than those which could be obtained from dealers. The Treasure Trove Regulations protect persons who sell antiquities to the Academy against claims from the Crown. Antiquities lose much of their value and interest if scraped, broken, or [illegible]. They should always be sent exactly as found, without any attempt at cleaning, and accompanied by a written statement of the locality and circumstances of their discovery. The Irish antiquities which it is desirable to preserve comprise ancient articles of gold, silver, bronze, or brass, iron, bone, and also cinerary urns, [illegible] stones, celts, flint arrowheads, etc. Finders of antiquities should send them to the Royal Irish Academy House, 19, Dawson Street, Dublin, and communicate by letter with the secretary. Expenses connected with the forwarding and carriage of the articles will be paid by the Academy. Persons who so desire can transmit articles through the constabulary of their localities. The antiquities acquired by the Academy are exhibited in the museum." I also hand in a letter which is sent to the Lord-Lieutenant as to any articles of treasure trove:—

"Treasure Trove,
"Royal Irish Academy,
19, Dawson Street, Dublin.
"—— of ——, 189 .

"Sir,—I beg to set forth on the other side hereof the particulars of decisions of the Committee of Antiquities of the Academy relative to the articles of treasure trove considered by them at their meeting on the   last.
I have the honour to be, sir,
"Your obedient servant,
"Secretary to said Committee.
"To the Under Secretary, Dublin Castle."

The notice to finders we have distributed extensively among the Constabulary and the schools in order to show the people generally what the nature of treasure trove is, and how [illegible] we find ourselves bound to insist on these articles of treasure trove coming to us.

267. That deals with antiquities generally—flint arrowheads, cinerary urns, and so forth?—This is intended for the schools, and generally for the people throughout Ireland altogether, so that they should understand that we are the proper persons to whom to take these articles. I have here a copy of the Treasury Minute which guides the whole thing. It is dated 10th July, 1860:—"Write to the solicitor with reference to his report of the 15th November last and subsequent communications on the subject of treasure trove, that my lords, agreeing with him in the tenor of his remarks with reference to the Home Office circular, have requested that it may be rescinded, and that it seems desirable now that such a notification should be issued as has thereof as will effect the object contemplated by this Board when the circular of the Home Office was first suggested. It appears from the statement of the solicitor that the process by which the rights of the Crown to treasure trove can be established is difficult and expensive, and it would seldom happen that the value of treasure trove recovered would repay the cost of recovery. The object my lords had in view in their proceedings with reference to this matter was to induce parties who may be finders of treasure, and who frequently belong to the labouring class, instead of selling the treasure, as is often the case, under the apprehension that it may be claimed at less than its intrinsic or metallic value, to the nearest public-house keeper or silversmith, in whose hands it is likely to be melted down, to bring or transmit it to some person authorised on the part of the Crown to receive it, and to receive to the finder its ascertained intrinsic or metallic value. My lords are of opinion that they would not be justified in going further than this. In many cases it must happen that treasure trove possesses no value whatever beyond the value of the metal composing it, and even in the cases of treasure possessing greater value as an object of antiquarian or historical interest, it would be difficult to ascertain correctly such value, and it would scarcely come within the province of this Board to become the purchasers of rare and curious coins. It seems probable that if it were generally known by the class of persons who usually are the finders of treasure that, by bringing it to some recognised officer such as the stipendiary of police, they would be sure to secure the metallic value from the Crown, to whom the treasure rightfully belongs, it would in many cases be sold to the Government, and assuming the metallic value only to be given for it, no loss would arise even if the treasure possessed no value beyond that of the metal. On the other hand, should it possess antiquarian value it would remain for this Board to deal with it in such manner as may appear desirable, either by allowing it at an intrinsic value to the British Museum or to some local museum, in which case the treasure would be preserved and become available as an object of interest without loss being sustained by the public. Cases would no doubt occur in which persons finding rare and valuable coins would dispose of them at higher prices than their intrinsic value. For such cases it would be desirable to make provision, as the treasure would find its way into some collection either public or private. In any circular to be now issued it will be proper that the correct and plain description should be given of the term 'treasure trove' and of the objects which fall within that denomination. It should be stated that the superintendent or inspector has been authorised to receive treasure trove, that it will be his duty to forward same with a report of the circumstances of the discovery to the solicitor of the Treasury, that the intrinsic value of the treasure will be ascertained at the Mint, and that my lords will remit the amount to the finders by the agency of the police." There is one point connected with that which is most valuable, namely, that the state in which the articles are found should be clearly set down. I feel very strongly, as interested in antiquarian subjects, the necessity of having all the circumstances of the find clearly laid down.

268. Is that a Treasury Minute issued from the Treasury here in London?—Yes, this is an exact copy that I had made for this purpose. I was saying that my feeling in respect of this matter, the necessity of having this thing done in the ordinary way, was this:—In reading the account of the find given in Mr. Evans's paper, which was an admirable account, so far as the archaeology of the thing was concerned, I found it did not contain any statement of what the exact position was in which the objects were found. I could not find out whether the boat was crumpled up or whether it was found intact. So far as I could find out, the ground was not dug up in order to ascertain whether there were any bones there.

269. How do you apply that to the subject of the enquiry?—In this way—if it were allowed to pass that the finder could himself, in any way, [illegible] up the circumstances of the discovery, it would be almost impossible in the future that archaeological science should be advanced at all. On the discovery of the things they ought to be let alone and then investigated by proper persons, and the details investigated which lead to a proper hypothesis; and that has not been done in this case. I never heard any arguments from anybody that this was not treasure trove, but however that may be, that is rather a matter for discussion before a learned body than for discussion before this Committee.

270. Now you have said that questions were asked in the House of Commons. What followed from that?—It was left on that basis so far as I could learn. I think there was nothing further done about the matter. It had to remain over. The question was asked whether the objects could not be handed over to the Royal Irish Academy, and it was stated that that could not be done unless a special Act were passed. Therefore we had to wait till Mr. Redmond's Bill was brought forward, and it was a perpetual wait till your Committee was promised and appointed.

271. Then is there nothing else you wish to say about the form, reference to us, "the circumstances under which these articles were discovered"?—I think not. The point I want to emphasise strongly is that the Academy was perfectly satisfied, so far as its judgment was concerned, that these were objects of treasure trove. It was quite certain, so far as the law by which it had always been

[illegible] was concerned, that the articles would go to the Academy for valuation and subsequently for deposit in our Museum; it was equally certain that treasure trove objects could not be for sale; and we knew nothing about the sale. Then when it was found out that they were treasure trove it was needless for us to act, because it was no use moving the Crown Solicitor, seeing that the Attorney General had himself had the circumstances before him. Consequently we concluded that we should trust to the justice of Parliament that the matter would be determined on a right-ful basis; but the Academy felt very strongly the necessity of having its claims generally brought before the public, so that they might see that this particular right and privilege with regard to treasure trove should be properly adhered to. I felt very strongly that the Academy as an institution connected with antiquarian objects should have a perfectly definite and assured position in this matter, particularly seeing that we have a good museum, one that is well looked after, and so far a collection of Celtic gold ornaments as is to be found anywhere.

872. Do you mean to say that the collection of gold ornaments in the Royal Irish Academy is in your judgment—apart from national feeling—of equal importance to a third party as the collection in the British Museum?—Yes, as Celtic objects.

873. Because they have a great many gold ornaments that you do not obtain?—That is so, they have some that we could not alter.

874. Before you go away from the circumstances under which these articles were offered for sale to the British Museum, and your action in the matter, I want to ask you this—was there any notice in any publications which would naturally come under your view, such as the [illegible] papers that are published, and so on? After the time that these articles were bought by the Museum and before the time that the matter was debated in Parliament, was there any notice published that the articles had gone into the custody of the British Museum?—No, I knew nothing about it. If I had thought that there was any possibility of their being disposed of I should certainly have moved the Academy.

875. Do you want to say anything more on that branch of the inquiry?—I think not.

876. Then the second head of reference is, "to consider and suggest regulations for avoiding undue competition between museums supported out of public funds in Scotland and Ireland on the one hand and the British Museum on the other, for the acquisition of objects of antiquarian and historical interest"?—With respect to that I have nothing to say, because I stand simply on the footing that these articles were treasure trove that ought by right to come to us. We should never enter into competition for them, but as treasure trove we have an absolute right to them; at all events by prescription and arrangement we consider that we have that right.

877. But apart from the question of this particular find of gold ornaments the reference here is as to general regulations, not necessarily affecting this particular case. I will put it in this way. Would you be in favour of the establishment of regulations for the purpose [illegible] [illegible] for avoiding undue competition between institutions supported out of public funds?—Certainly.

878. Have you had any instances, in your own experience, of such undue competition?—No, I think not, because we are too poor to compete with almost anybody for anything, and therefore we do not compete. It is a very limited sum of money that we have. Often we feel ourselves in a difficulty, and then when anything really valuable comes up we have to ask the Government to help us in some manner.

879. How much is the sum you have?—Only £100 a year is given for treasure trove.

880. Not for the purchase of other articles apart from treasure trove?—That is a question generally of the private funds of the Academy. We have very great expenses; we are a publishing body, and often we have a very limited sum at our command. Up to the last two years the sum of £100 was ear-marked for her, but since then a Grant-in-Aid has been given us generally for general management expenses, publications, and so forth.

881. Then, how have you acquired the valuable collection of gold ornaments?—We have had that a good many years, but we have had to divide it. On one occasion we bought a collection for £150. Of course, there we had to spread the payment over several years.

Prof. R. [illegible], LL.D.

[illegible], 1898.

882. Then the £100 a year accumulates; you get £100 every year, whether you spend it or not in the particular year?—At first we were rather limited enough to send the money back when it was not expended. Then we applied that it might be allowed to lap over, and we were allowed to do that. Of course, it could not be held that we were always obliged to spend strictly up to the limitation of the amount. It was done as carefully and even parsimoniously as could be. The money had to be made to go as far as it would.

883. We were told by Mr. Read and Sir Edward Thompson that the relations between the authorities of the British Museum and the authorities of the Royal Irish Academy had, until this occurrence which we have been dealing with, been of a very friendly character?—I have nothing to say against that. I have no distinct recollection of any relations at all, but I am sure that they were not unfriendly. We are all interested in the maintenance of our respective antiquities.

884. Sir Edward Thompson mentioned one case in which, by the intervention of Sir Wollaston Franks, notice was given to the Irish Academy that a certain collection was to be had, and it was obtained—I do not know exactly under what circumstances. Do you remember that case?—I think I have heard that there was a case in point, but I am sure that the relations were friendly, and I could not have believed them otherwise. I am quite prepared to accept that. I could not think that any one at the British Museum would envy us our little treasures.

885. Do you think that there should be a regulation as regards articles of value which come to the knowledge of the authorities of the British Museum, as to articles to be had in England, or reciprocally articles which might be acquirable in Ireland or Scotland respectively, that notice ought to be given by the authorities of each of those museums to the authorities of the museum of the country to which the articles ought, for some reason or other, be supposed especially to belong?—No; I would rather leave it very much on the basis on which it has been hitherto, namely, that when articles which are natural to one country, and plainly belong to one country, are found in it, they should be preserved in the Museum of that country. If it cannot be determined whether the article belongs to A or B, then friendly correspondence might be interchanged, so that there might be no avoidance of any competition. It seems to me that as regards treasure trove the arrangements now are quite good.

886. I was not speaking of treasure trove objects; I was speaking of other articles, which might become available for a purchaser, be the purchaser who he might?—I should not be in favour of making any regulations in that case. I would rather leave it to the feeling of friendliness, which should naturally prevail between public bodies.

887. (Sir T. Esmonde.) In the case of historic curiosities?—In the case of historic curiosities that were plainly Irish, then I should say that it would be very eminently desirable that they should come to Ireland, and I should be willing, of course, that it should be made a regulation that that should be so; but it is not always determinable beforehand that objects are specially Irish. Sometimes objects may have been British; sometimes they may have been Scandinavian.

888. (Chairman.) Take the particular case of this discovery of ornaments. Suppose the circumstances of discovery had been such as not to warrant them as treasure trove, as you believe, and as in this particular instance appears to have been the case; but under other circumstances, still, that they had been found in Ireland, or had been in Ireland for a long time, or had some connection with some old house or family in Ireland—I am only suggesting cases to you—suppose the articles had been brought by some person, for sale to the British Museum, as these articles were brought, would you be in favour of a notice being given by the British Museum that such articles were for sale, before they proceeded to deal with them themselves?—On one condition, I would. Here is the difficulty. Let us suppose that these particular objects here were proved not to have been treasure trove; that will make a definite case. Then suppose the British Museum had sent to the Academy a notice declaring that on such and such a date if you do not present arguments to show that it is more desirable that you should have them, we will purchase them. I should be quite willing, if there were

Prof. R. Atkinson, LL.D.

13 Dec. 1898

and a competition in the prices—that is to say, if the Academy was allowed then, when it had its opinion, to place a price on the things, so that they should come to us; but if the potential vendor were to say, "No, you have only offered £500, and the British Museum have offered £600," such a proposal would be nugatory, because we have not the wealth of the British Museum, and perhaps we have not so public spirit. We may not have been willing to put our hands into our pockets to that extent. So that I think that would be nugatory, unless it was put in the category of treasure trove, and by one assigning a price to it ourselves. If the British Museum are allowed to assign a price that might be more than we were prepared to go to, that would cut us out altogether.

288. (Sir John Lubbock.) Then, besides the British Museum, there may be other purchasers—private purchasers in this country, or purchasers for America: they will have to be considered also?—Certainly. I was going to say, if Mr. Day had dared—I use that word advisedly—to put a public advertisement in the papers, or to send to America, I have no doubt he could have run up the price of these articles to £1,000. There are dealers who would have given £2,000 for these absolutely invaluable objects. I am not quite sure that if I were a wealthy man, I would not give £1,000 for the lot myself. So that, when you come to competition prices, the theory is untenable.

289. (Chairman.) That was not the idea that I had in my mind. I was putting it to you, whether private notice could not be given by the authorities of one museum to the authorities of another as to articles not necessarily of such a great price that you could not compete for them—that notice should be given so as to afford opportunity to the museum of the country to which the articles, presumably, should belong, of purchasing the articles before the authorities of the museum to whom they have been brought for sale proceeded to buy themselves. Of course, there is no good giving notice if you have not got money to buy some very valuable things, or if you have not got any opportunity of appealing to the Treasury or anybody else to find money for the purpose. But take the case of articles which are not of such extreme value as that, which you would be able to purchase at a fair price?—But the difficulty would be to assign the fair price, because the vendor might say, "You have offered me £50, and the British Museum say that they will give me £60." It is clear that it would be futile to offer the thing to us in those circumstances. We might be willing to purchase the object, and be very glad to get it, but we might not be willing to give the price which the British Museum, out of its enormous purse, is able and willing to give.

290. (Sir John Lubbock.) And would there not be the danger that a rich American might step in, and give £80 or £100?—There is that danger, too.

291. (Chairman.) The other part of our reference is, "And for ensuring that, in the case of objects which, from their origin and associations, are of peculiar interest either to Scotland or Ireland, the museum so interested should be afforded an opportunity of purchasing them before they are acquired by any other institution supported out of public funds." As I understand, you do not attach importance to that?—Not unless we have the right to purchase them at our price, because, otherwise, it would be very little use.

292. (Sir T. Esmonde.) But if there was no competition between the different museums?—In that case, I should heartily agree. The thing is to prevent competition. If some competent person should assign the price, I should be very glad. I think objects found in Ireland, which are clearly of Irish interest, should come to us in Ireland. I am very strongly of that opinion.

293. Do you think it would not be possible for the heads of the various museums to communicate in these matters, without the dealers or the public generally knowing anything about it?—That might be possible, but my experience hardly enables me to give a competent judgment upon that. I do not see how that can be done, and I have not had sufficient experience of that matter to know whether it would be advisable. I still feel the danger that, unless there were a right of absolute preservation on the part of the country on whose territories the objects were found, it might be futile to them, because they could not afford it.

294. (Chairman.) Is not that rather a different question? I think it is the practice as between the Society of Antiquaries in Scotland and the Treasury that, besides the ordinary Vote which is given to the Society, they have a right—at all events, they make it a practice—in cases where the object they desire to secure for their museum is beyond the reach of their resources, to apply to the Treasury, with the self-confidence apparently of obtaining funds from them for the special purpose. Have you any such habit or practice as regards the Irish Academy?—Yes, we did apply to the Government on previous occasions. In fact, it was in that way that we received the Tara Brooch, and the Ardagh Chalice, and the Shrine of St. Lachtin.

295. Then suppose you got notice, say, from the British Museum, or the Society of Antiquaries in Scotland, that some treasures, as they would be for the Irish Academy, were available; why should not you apply to the Government?—I should be very glad if there were a regulation of that kind, if it were understood that the British Museum would not interfere with our purchase, or with any application to the Government to have them purchased for us at a favourable figure.

297. Your view, then, is that the reason you do not think a regulation of the kind that we have been discussing would be of any very great service to you is because after all you might be defeated by the competition of, we will say, the British Museum or some other museum?—Exactly.

298. But the words of the reference here are as I have read them out to you, "to suggest regulations for avoiding undue competition"?—Those regulations, I think, would have to be made by more competent persons than I.

299. Suppose such regulations could be made by any person, would you be in favour of regulations for such a purpose?—If I saw them and approved of the regulations, yes. As a matter of general principle I am in favour of regulation. My only difficulty is that I do not see how it is to be done, but if regulations can be made I should give them careful consideration and form a definite opinion. I can only say broadly that I am in favour if possible of having things done without competition, and if such a scheme of regulations be drawn up I should certainly give them a most favourable judgment, so as if I possibly could to say yes to them heartily.

300. But your main objection to the drawing up of such regulations, as I understand, is that the effect of notice being given to you would be likely to be defeated by the superior purse of the British Museum to buy?—Just so, that is my one and sole objection. I am quite willing to have the thing dealt, so, by regulations.

301. Then suppose there were regulations in the first place that notice should be given to the body locally interested, and in the second place a regulation, if one could be devised, to prevent undue competition between these bodies, would you be in favour of that?—Yes, always with the proviso that it did not touch the existing treasure trove regulations, I would be in favour of the principle that your lordship has mentioned.

302. There is a third head of reference to us "to consider whether any, and if so, what, relaxations should be made in the regulations which prevent the British Museum from parting with objects which it has once acquired?"—There, my lord, I am perfectly helpless. I do not know the regulations of the British Museum. I am only strongly of opinion personally that these objects ought to come to us.

303. But what is pointed at here is that there is a statute which prevents the British Museum from parting with any objects which have once come into its custody, with two exceptions, namely when the articles are duplicates or are for some reason unfit for preservation in their collection. Now take the case of this collection of Irish gold ornaments, if your contention as to treasure trove is well founded, no question, because as regards that particular collection you would get it back according to your contention by force of law?—Exactly.

304. But assuming that that contention did not prevail, and that it was not treasure trove, so that the British Museum had acquired a title by purchase in spite of its having originally been treasure trove, in that case, even supposing the British Museum were desirous of returning those objects to you they would be prohibited from doing so under this statute. Would you be in favour of the relaxation or the alteration in some way of that legal obligation on the British Museum to keep objects that they have once acquired whether they like it or not?—I should be in favour of a relaxation of any or every kind to get the objects into our museum where I deliberately and positively think they ought to come, but I hold that primâ facie they are treasure trove, and belong to us by law. The Attorney-General very distinctly expressed himself

of that opinion, and I think there can be no doubt about the matter.

305. It is conceivable that there might be some objects in the British Museum which you would like to have in the Irish Academy, and which the Trustees of the British Museum would be willing to part with, say, in exchange for some article that you have in the Irish Academy. In such a case as that the British Museum are precluded from entertaining such an idea, quite apart from any question of treasure trove. I am not speaking of treasure trove, but something which is not treasure trove. As the law stands at present, be they ever so willing to exchange with you some article that they have for some article that you have, they have no power to do it under that statute?—Does your lordship ask me whether in my opinion any relaxation in general of that statute should be made?

306. Yes?—I think not. I think it is good that once objects are acquired by the British Museum they should remain there. I think that is a fair and reasonable thing. I do not want to have the possibility, in fact, of the bigger body, or anybody coming to us in the Royal Irish Academy and saying: "Will you exchange this for that?" I do not like that idea. Anything having been bought fairly and squarely before the world ought to remain with the museum that has purchased it. I do not want any movement so far as I am concerned—but here I am giving only my own personal opinion,—I do not want any movement to get these objects back if they are not ours by legal right.

307. I am not speaking now of the question of treasure trove. That is not the point I am on, but suppose some object that is not treasure trove—I suppose you have objects in your museum which are not there as treasure trove?—Yes.

308. Suppose you had an object which you were desirous to part with in exchange for something which the British Museum had—I am not putting the case that there should be any right of claim on your part that you could insist upon, but suppose two bodies were perfectly willing to exchange with one another certain objects, do you think it is desirable that in such a case as that the law should prevent such an exchange from being carried out?—In general, yes, and for this reason. Objects have not the same [illegible] at different times in different [illegible]. It might very possibly happen that at a particular time a committee who had charge of a particular article would not see the value, let us say, of Celtic ornaments in general, and might be willing to exchange them for anything that would make a pretty show. I would hold that once in the museum they should remain there.

309. Is there anything else you wish to say?—I think not. I think your lordship's courtesy has enabled me to say everything I wished.

310. (*Sir John Lubbock.*) Have you had before you the report made by Sir Edward Thompson as to the exact circumstances under which these Celtic ornaments and other objects were bought by the British Museum?—No.

311. Then, I should like just to put on record the exact facts. I will read you the exact evidence that Sir Edward Thompson laid before us, and ask you whether you agree that that evidence states the facts. Sir Edward Thompson told us: "In the autumn of 1896, Mr. Robert Day, F.S.A., a well-known collector of works of art and antiquities, living at Cork, informed Mr. C. H. Read, the keeper of the British and Mediæval Antiquities in the British Museum, that he had secured from a silversmith some very fine gold ornaments of the late Celtic work. Mr. Read, who is also the secretary of the Society of Antiquaries of London, suggested to Mr. Day that the Society should have an opportunity of seeing them. Accordingly, Mr. Day exhibited the ornaments at a meeting of the society, on the 14th January, 1897, and an account of the meeting appeared in the *Athenæum* newspaper, of the 30th January. Meanwhile, Mr. Read having expressed an opinion to Mr. Day, that these important objects should pass to the British Museum, should he at any time part with them, negotiations followed, with the result that Mr. Day offered the collection to the trustees of the British Museum for the sum of £600. Mr. Read recommended the purchase to the trustees in a report of the 5th April, 1897, a copy of which is herein annexed. The trustees sanctioned the purchase at a meeting of the Standing Committee on the 8th April, 1897, the order for payment was issued on the 12th May." I think that that substantially agrees with what you have told us?—Yes.

312. I wish to ascertain whether that is a fair statement of the circumstances?—I think that is perfectly right.

313. Then I do not understand that, so far as regards the action of the Trustees of the British Museum, you make any complaint against them in this matter?—Yes, I do. 13

314. Will you kindly explain to the Committee in what respect you think they are to blame?—Take this paragraph: "Mr. Read having expressed an opinion to Mr. Day that these important objects should pass to the British Museum, should he at any time part with them." What I cannot understand is that these objects could have been purchased without knowledge on the part of the British Museum authorities that they were found under circumstances which *primâ facie* forced upon everybody reading Mr. Evans's paper the opinion that they were treasure trove. If they were treasure trove, it was not a question of Mr. Day parting with them, but a question of his right to have them at all. If I had been in the service of the British Museum, and I had been approached, I should have said, "Mr. Day, how do you come by these gold ornaments at all?" I cannot understand how it is that no question of that kind was put to him. Here was the paper, that had been read by Mr. Read, stating that these things had been found by a farmer who turned up the subsoil, and discovered them. How could anybody think that they had a right to purchase those articles until the question whether they were treasure trove was disposed of? That must have arisen, *primâ facie*, in the mind of anybody. I cannot understand how the British Museum could have acted as they did. That is my difficulty.

315. Then, according to you, everything which is of gold or silver which is found in Ireland is treasure trove?—Not quite so; but everything that is found under such circumstances as these—struck by a ploughman under the subsoil in that particular way.

316. Will you kindly explain, for my information, under what circumstances a gold or silver ornament found in Ireland would be treasure trove, and when it would not, in your opinion?—That I could not do until I have a more elaborate description of the law of treasure trove given by some competent authority—which I sincerely hope I shall get—but I have the opinion here of Sir Robert Finlay, given in 1892, which I should just like to read to you.

317. (*Sir Herbert Maxwell.*) Is that in Ireland?—No. This is extracted from the proceedings of the Society of Antiquaries of London. "A labourer digging in a field struck with his hoe something hard, which proved to be a gold ring. There was no other object of antiquity found in the neighbourhood. The ring was claimed by the lady of the manor, and given by her to the clergyman of the parish. The labourer who found it was rewarded. A superintendent of police called on behalf of the Treasury, who claimed it as treasure trove. The clergyman, without disputing the right of the Crown, sent it up to the Treasury." That is a parallel case.

318. (*Mr. John Morley.*) Is that an Irish case?—No, it is in London. Then I have here the opinion of Sir Robert Finlay and Mr. George H. Blakesley, dated 5th April, 1892, which lays it down in words far better than I could use: "We are of opinion that the ring could not under the circumstances be rightly called treasure trove, because it does not appear to have been placed where it was found by any person desirous of hiding it," that was the argument. "We think that according to the authorities (see, for instance, 3rd inst. 132-3) there must be presumptive evidence of hiding in order to bring an object under the claim of the Crown as treasure trove." Now comes the point. "No doubt in most cases the circumstances of the finding must be the only basis of any presumption of hiding; as, for instance, if a number of articles are found collected together in a vase, or buried in a manner inconsistent with their having got into their position through an accident." Now, when I saw these objects—a heterogeneous mass of things—a boat, complete, as I am informed, a torc, chains, and various other things—a heterogeneous mass of objects brought together to a mass and hidden under the ground, where they were found by a ploughman, I could not infer that these things had got there by an accident. It seems to me that presumably, *primâ facie*, this was a case absolutely parallel with what Sir Robert Finlay and Mr. George H. Blakesley were describing. They say, "The circumstances of the finding must be the sole basis of any presumption of hiding." Therefore it seems to me that anyone holding that these things were not treasure trove, must show some fair ground for that opinion.

Prof. [illegible], M.D.

19 Dec. 1898.

[illegible], some rare cases, under which a man could say that these things got there by accident. To me it was a case of [illegible] Judaei Apella. I cannot imagine that anyone could believe that they got there by accident. What occurs to me is that the way they got there was in quite the normal fashion. This was the plunder of some one, hidden secretly when the plunderer was setting out on some fresh depredation; that he was probably killed—the normal fate of plunderers in the North of Ireland at that time—and the things remained hidden for centuries. But to say that they happened to be there by accident—never! Mr. Evans, in his capital paper, only turned my objection when he came to his general conclusions, because he said it was a votive deposit, and I could not see any argument for that. But here you have the opinion of these eminent counsel, in which they put an exactly parallel case—"as, for instance, if a number of articles are found collected together in a vase, or buried in a manner inconsistent with their having got into their position through an accident." I could not conceive that these particular things got there "through an accident."

519. (*Sir Herbert Maxwell.*) If the boat, for instance, had been recorded, that might have been an accident?—If it had been a sailing boat; but this is a gold model of a boat.

520. (*Sir T. Esmonde.*) And these things were under the subsoil, which is rather important?—Yes, because they were turned up by the ploughshare. In fact, everything seemed to make for this present case.

521. (*Sir John Lubbock.*) I need not pursue the matter further with you. The law of treasure trove is rather complicated, and no purpose would be served by my entering into a legal and technical argument with you. I suppose you would hardly regard it as desirable that we should have no Irish or Scotch gold ornaments in the British Museum, or that there should be no Irish gold ornaments in Scotland, and so on. You would not, as an archaeologist, consider that everything found in Ireland should be confined to Ireland, and everything found in Scotland should be confined to Scotland, and everything found in England should be confined to England?—That is a very academic question.

522. It is a very important scientific question whether it is desirable or not that we should have in London an interesting collection of Irish objects. I ask you as an archaeologist rather than as an Irishman, if I may say so?—I would reply by asking you, Would not you think it desirable that we in Ireland should have the opportunity of comparing Irish objects of different periods?

523. If you decline to give me an answer I will not press you?—I do not decline, but I answer you in that way. It is much more natural, surely, that I should insist on our collection of objects being complete than that there should be an incomplete series of objects in two places. I would rather, for example, that you got everything of purely British work in the British Museum. I should, so far as possible, allow the museum of each country to have a perfect representation of all the nature of its ornaments, etc., that students might go there and study them. We have a number of torcs already in our Irish Museum, and it is important that the torc in this find should be with us for purposes of comparison.

524. I quite agree with you, if all you mean is that you ought to have a typical collection, and that we should have a typical collection; but if you tell me that you really think that you should have everything that is gold that is found in Ireland that is another matter. Your opinion is no doubt entitled to very great weight; I only want to arrive at it?—When you talk of a typical collection, I do not know what is typical; I want them complete.

525. In fact, you wish to have every gold ornament that is found in Ireland?—That is my opinion.

526. Now, in this particular case, you had before you the article in the *Athenaeum* of 28th January, 1897. Might I ask why you did not then take steps to claim the articles as treasure trove, because you knew the articles were in Mr. Day's possession?—It is had immediately done so. The moment the article came out I went to Sir Patrick Coll and asked him to move the authorities to find out who the finder was. He categorically told me that he had no means of putting the law into operation until I indicated to him who the finder was, and the place, and the time of the find.

527. Did not you communicate with Mr. Day?—No.

528. Was not there a great danger that, between January, 1897, and March, 1898, Mr. Day might have sold these articles to which you attached, very justly, so much importance, to America or elsewhere?—I had the professional confidence in the law reaching him in that case, because I believe that, *primâ facie*, there was a legal right in these articles as treasure trove.

529. Suppose he had sold them to America?—In that case I should have put the law in operation and let the law demonstrate its efficiency. It would at all events have made it clear to the people of Ireland that these objects ought to be brought to us.

530. The law gives a right to the Crown to take the articles at perhaps much less than their real value; but surely the law would not involve any punishment to Mr. Day for having sold them to an American collector?—I think so.

531. Do you mean to say he could have been punished if he had sold them to an American or Continental collector?—I rather think it would be a misdemeanour; but I am not a lawyer. But then I say, that if I had known the name of the finder, Mr. Thomas Nicholl, I would have put the law into operation.

532. But why did you not communicate with Mr. Day? Mr. Day's name was mentioned when Mr. Evans' paper was read at the Society of Antiquaries?—The articles were in his possession.

533. What was to prevent Mr. Day in the meantime selling them to America?—I regard him as being illegally in possession of these things. I would not have asked my own brother for these objects under those circumstances. I hold that Mr. Day knew that what he was doing was an infraction of the law, because his attention had been called to it in a perfectly parallel case two years before.

534. Do I understand that you think that supposing Mr. Day had sold these articles to an American collector or some other collector the law could in any way have punished him for so doing?—I think so.

535. Now let me put this to you. There is a law which you say enables the Royal Irish Academy to purchase articles, gold or silver. You assume that they know the name of the person who has them, they are to purchase them at their bullion value, although, as a matter of practice, they give rather more?—That has been our practice.

536. Now, do you think really that it is in the interests of science that a person who finds an article of this description is to be told that he must take it to one place where he will only get one-third or one-quarter of its value, and that if he should part with it to anybody at the fair market price he is liable to be punished?—I do not say that he would get only one-third of the value. The value is difficult to determine. I was referring to the bullion value. I can only talk about the value of the thing intrinsically. We generally give them two or three times the intrinsic value.

537. I only wish to ascertain what your opinion is; you and I are both archaeologists; what we want is the promotion of archaeological science. As I understand you, the law as it at present stands—I confess I am rather surprised to hear it, is that the Royal Irish Academy is to give the bullion value, or if they are generously so pleased, something more; and that if a person found that he could sell the articles for a higher value he is liable to be punished hereafter if he does so?—Yes.

538. Surely the natural tendency of that is that anybody finding an interesting article will sell it; people will not again go and read a paper before the Society of Antiquaries and exhibit the articles. Do you think that that is in the interests of archaeological science?—Yes, I do most thoroughly, because in a country like Ireland, where the people are very ignorant——

539. But very intelligent?—Intelligent, no doubt; but where they are very ignorant about the circumstances of the case, it may easily happen that a dealer would go to the people and tell them: "The value of this is about £5, but I will give you £25 for it." I believe what happened in this matter was that the finder was perfectly unconscious of the amount he might have got. I do not know what it was, but it was a small sum that he got compared with £600. And I say that those ignorant people should not be imposed upon in that manner. It is better, until the spread of education shall have shown them precisely what the circumstances of archaeological science are, that they should be defended against dealers

Prof. R. Atkinson, LL.D.

13 Dec. 1898.

purchasing articles from them for very considerably less than their value.

340. I will put this to you again: your contention is, under the law as it stands, whether rightly or wrongly, that your Royal Irish Academy can insist on having these objects both from the British Museum?—I think so.

341. You have admitted that Mr. Day during the year and a quarter after these exhibitions might have sold them to America, although he might have incurred some penalty in doing so?—Yes.

342. Then, do not you think the British Museum exercised a wise discretion in preserving these objects for at any rate one of our national institutions?—No, I think what they might have been expected to do, and what I should have done in similar circumstances would have been to inform the Royal Irish Academy that these objects were in the market.

343. The Royal Irish Academy, you have already admitted, knew by the article in the *Athenæum* that the objects were in Mr. Day's possession?—They did not know that the objects were for sale.

344. They knew that Mr. Day had bought these objects, and that he was a dealer. Was it not a natural inference that he bought them for sale?—No, on the contrary. My conversations that Mr. Day had been forced two years before to give up objects precisely in the same way made me say, "He will not dare to sell these objects now until the matter is decided"; therefore, I confess I had not the slightest idea that it was possible he should have sold them.

345. (*Mr. John Morley.*) Did not you speak to Mr. Day at all?—Never.

346. (*Sir John Lubbock.*) I believe it is the case that our collection of these early Celtic ornaments is not so good as the collection that you have in Dublin?—I think not.

347. I presume you would agree that it would be natural that the keeper of this department of the British Museum would wish under these circumstances to improve our collection of early Celtic ornaments?—Quite so. If I had been he I should probably have done the same thing. It is very natural; it is, of course, another question whether it is legally right or wrong. I hold that he was not legally justified in doing it, but it was quite natural that he should wish to get them for the purpose of improving his collection.

348. If it was natural that they should wish to improve their collection, why should you be so much surprised, considering that a year and a half elapsed, during which the Irish authorities did nothing, that the British Museum decided to acquire them?—I cannot admit that the Irish authorities did nothing. We did everything we could.

349. What did you do?—We went to the Crown Solicitor, and we found we had to wait till Parliament met.

350. There was no question of Parliament about it. Here is the law; it is not for Parliament to put the law in operation. If Mr. Day had these objects, surely you are the custodians of these matters in Ireland, and it was natural that you should go to Mr. Day and enquire of him who found them?—No, even on the previous occasion I did not move; it was only when the constabulary informed us. If I found that anybody had in their possession treasure trove, whensoever derived, I should still say it was for the constabulary to put the law in motion.

351. Then, may I ask why you did not move the constabulary?—Because it is the constabulary who must take the initiative. On this occasion I had no data on which to move whatever; I had no legal power; I could only ask the Crown Solicitor. We have to deal entirely with the Irish Government.

352. At any rate, you have already stated in your evidence that from January of one year to April of the following year nothing was done in the matter?—Nothing could be done. In the thorough belief that we had that this was treasure trove, and therefore it would come to us under the natural process of law, we were quite satisfied with that.

353. Then your idea was that these objects mostly or [illegible] must gravitate to you?—I would not say gravitate, but that they must come to us by the natural process of law. The moment Parliament reached it——

354. Why should Parliament have anything to do with it?—In order to find out the finder.

355. That is not the duty of Parliament?—It is the privilege of Parliament. If I had put a notice in the paper about this find I would have been liable to all sorts of attacks.

356. Then why did not you bring it before Parliament in 1897?—Because I had placed it in the hands of the Crown Solicitor. I asked him to move the constabulary to find out the name of the finder and the place and circumstances of the find. It seemed to me, and it still seems to me, that that was the normal way. I should do exactly the same thing again.

357. Then it comes practically to this, that in your judgment the authorities of the British Museum should buy nothing of gold or silver found in Ireland, because being treasure trove it belongs to the Royal Irish Academy, and ought to go to them?—I would not quite say that, but being found under circumstances which presumptively make it certain that they are treasure trove, they ought to come to us.

358. If the authorities of the British Museum think a thing is not treasure trove in your judgment they are entitled to purchase it; if they think it is treasure trove they are bound not to purchase it?—Not quite. If they think that it is not treasure trove, and they can prove that in a court of law, yes; but it will not do if they simply think it is not treasure trove.

359. As a practical man I will ask you this. In the case of an article found in Ireland, how are the British Museum to prove in a court of law that it is not treasure trove?—They are to take the presumptions of the case, and the presumptions in the matter of this particular find that the articles were treasure trove appeared to me to have been absolutely unanswerable from the very circumstances of the discovery of the find.

360. Then I will take it in this way, that unless it has been proved in a court of law that the article is not treasure trove, nothing in gold or silver that is found in Ireland is to be bought by the authorities of the British Museum?—But under the circumstances here there could be no doubt that they were treasure trove.

361. And therefore ought not to be purchased by the British Museum?—Certainly.

362. Then we are to have in the British Museum no representatives of Irish art except such as has been proved in a court of law not to be treasure trove; is that the view which you wish to lay before the Committee?—Well, I think almost I would say yes. If they are Irish art they should appear in Ireland.

363. Up to the time of this last controversy about this find of gold ornaments there has been no friction between the British Museum and the Royal Irish Academy?—None whatever, and on the contrary we have always had the assistance of Sir Edward Thompson in various things. Everything has gone on as on rails. I could not believe that there was any ill feeling on the part of the British Museum to us, not a particle.

364. (*Sir T. Esmonde.*) Are you aware if in foreign countries there are any regulations which prevent antiquities being taken out of the country?—I do not know that.

365. In reference to these gold ornaments, do you consider that they filled any vacancy in the Irish collection?—Yes, and no. As I said, they are a mixed lot. With reference to the boat, it is undoubtedly very valuable; the chain I am not so sure about; the boat is rather odd [illegible].

366. Do you consider that they would or would not fill a vacancy in the British Museum?—I would not say that, because I am not so familiar with the objects in the British Museum, and do not know exactly what its wants are. Those who know the British Museum might argue the contrary from their side, but I really do not exactly know what their collection is.

367. Then in reference to treasure trove generally found in Ireland, you do not hold that no Irish treasure trove should be purchased by the British Museum, I take it?—I am afraid I do.

368. Subject to this: suppose that treasure trove were found which the Royal Irish Academy did not wish to possess—suppose it had duplicates, for instance—would you object to that treasure trove going to the British Museum with the goodwill of the Irish Academy?—Duplicate is a very vague term. I would have every "duplicate" that I could get of objects where art is individual, because they are not duplicates. This is not a case of Manchester machine productions; the articles

Prof. R. Atkinson, LL.D.

13 June 1898.

[illegible] is shown on each separate ornament. We have got thousands of coins, but I would not give many out of them.

369. Do you think that all Irish treasure trove should remain in Ireland?—Quite so.

370. The British Museum has a very good collection of Irish gold ornaments?—Yes, and they might give back to us those that are Celtic.

371. Has there been a discrepancy as to the date of the finding of these gold ornaments. Sir Patrick Coll, I think, says that they were found some time in the spring of 1897, and the British Museum authorities say that they were found in the spring of 1896?—I have no knowledge as to when they were found, or the exact circumstances; my only knowledge is what is set out in Mr. Evans' paper at the beginning of "Archaeologia."

372. (Chairman.) It must have been in 1896, because they were exhibited on the 14th January, 1897.

372*. (Sir T. Esmonde.) Otherwise does not it seem very curious that the Irish Office should have no more information on the matter than they had?—In Ireland things go on so differently from the way they go on in England. We are very independent people, and do not like to inform. Now, I could have gone down to that place and found out probably all about the find, but I took good care not to do so. I thought that should be done by the constabulary.

373. And the constabulary did not do it?—No; why I do not know. I should like to ask Sir Patrick Coll why it was not done.

374. It is a matter of interest to know how that long delay came about?—I have never understood it.

375. Then with reference to the system of treasure trove, both in Ireland and in England, we had it in evidence the other day that in England the practice in the case of treasure trove is for the Treasury to inform the British Museum of the finding of treasure trove, and to ascertain from the British Museum if the British Museum wishes to secure the articles?—Yes.

376. That is the practice in England?—Yes.

377. From the facts of this special case evidently it is not the practice in Ireland?—No. Up to 1861 there had been [illegible] about the matter. A memorial had been sent forward, asking for certain privileges with regard to treasure trove, and then came the Treasury minute, of which I have read a copy, which regulated the practice in a certain manner. That sum of £100 was given, but it was paid through the constabulary altogether. In 1868 the Government gave us a treasure trove grant of £100 a year, but the action of the constabulary has always been to put us into operation when anything of a particular nature was discovered, and you can see by the notices to finders, to which I have referred, that we used every endeavour in our power to familiarise the people with the fact that we are the body concerned in the recovering of Irish antiquities.

378. I have lived a great many years in Ireland, but I must say that I have never seen that notice?—It is on all the constabulary notices. We had 20,000 of those notices printed some years ago. It was proposed that we should put them up in wood, but we had not the money. We did everything possible in our power to make it public property, that these objects should be brought to us.

379. In your opinion the constabulary might show a little more energy in regard to treasure trove?—I think so.

380. But I gather from you that the pressure in Ireland is, if I may put it, that the onus probandi rests with the Royal Irish Academy in the case of treasure trove?—I would scarcely put it in that way. The circumstances of the case have no onus probandi of themselves. We, I think, are not put to it to prove that in every case it is treasure trove.

381. But you are put to it to prove that the thing has been found?—Yes. Suppose I received a private letter to say that a find had been made in County Cork, I should write to the finder, and say, "Will you tell me the circumstances of the find?" For example, if I had known that Mr. Nichol had found these things, I should have written at once.

382. We had it in evidence that the British Museum had about £160,000 a year voted to it by Parliament, whereas the Royal Irish Academy got £100 a year?—Yes, but that is not quite a fair way of putting it. We get £2,000 a year; that is our Grant in Aid.

383. That is your total grant?—Yes; at first the £100 was earmarked for this purpose, but now we get a Grant in Aid, and can spend it more or less as we please, but I take it that the sum is practically earmarked yet.

384. (Chairman.) Besides that, you have told us that on one occasion you made an application to the Government, when you wanted to make a special purchase, which application they complied with?—Yes, in fact we have found everybody exceedingly willing to help us. The Tara Brooch, the Ardagh Chalice, and the Shrine of St. Lachtain were purchased in this way. We were helped most liberally.

385. (Sir John Lubbock.) In the Thames was comparing £160,000 with £2,000, but the £160,000 is for the whole expenditure of the British Museum, and of the Natural History Museum, not simply for the purchase of antiquarian objects?—No. It is impossible to make any parallel. I value the British Museum so immensely that I should not wish to introduce any comparisons of the kind.

386. (Sir T. Esmonde.) I wanted to know what your total resources were?—But then our needs are not so great. I am not dissatisfied with the amount that is given to us at all. I think it is relatively pretty fair. Perhaps I should like more for books, but considering that there are but so many objects to be bought, I am not willing to ask for more, because I am sure that in a special case we could ask with so much more force.

387. I think the general trend of the evidence the other day was that the responsibility for losing these ornaments rested with the Royal Irish Academy. Now, in this matter the Royal Irish Academy followed the usual regulations which it always follows?—Yes. I think I might answer that we could not have acted otherwise.

388. (Sir Herbert Maxwell.) Mr. Day is a Fellow of the Royal Irish Academy is he not?—No; he is a Fellow of the English Society of Antiquaries; he is a Member of the Royal Irish Academy, not a Fellow. We do not have Fellows there.

Mr. G. Coffey.

Mr. G. Coffey, called; and Examined.

389. (Chairman.) You are the Superintendent of Irish Antiquities in the Museum of the Science and Art Department in Dublin?—Yes.

390. Would you explain to the Committee exactly what are the regulations between the Royal Irish Academy and your Department as to the custody of these articles?—The collection of Irish antiquities was originally made by the Royal Irish Academy, and when the Government established the Museum Buildings in Dublin, they, with other bodies, deposited their collection in the new museum. Since that time the Academy still receive objects of antiquity presented to them; a very considerable number are so received from time to time, and they also purchase, under their grant for treasure trove, and these articles as they are received by the Academy are deposited in the Museum under my custody.

391. Have the Royal Irish Academy any museum of their own at the present time?—No; but under the terms of deposit the control and custody of the collection was reserved to them.

392. They have transferred the whole of their collection from where it was in Dawson Street into the building of the Science and Art Department?—Yes.

393. And it is there taken care of?—Yes.

394. Whose servants are the people who actually have charge of the collection?—The Science and Art Department.

395. But I suppose as to all matters of rearranging the collection or adding to the collection, the Royal Irish Academy would still be the controlling body?—They would in a measure have control.

396. Will you explain that to us, because we have been a little uncertain as to the exact relations between the two bodies?—The term "control and custody" has since been interpreted. As a matter of fact, to my appointment, the Academy were first consulted, being given what amounted to a nomination, but what, perhaps, in strictly legal terms, would not have been so—it was really a recommendation more than a nomination. The relations of the Academy and the Department have never been legally determined. The Academy have the right of visiting the Museum, and they could make recommenda-

Mr G. Coffey. 13 Dec 1898.

[illegible] to be any alteration in the arrangements, but I do not know that they could enforce them. The point has never arisen, and really the document is very vague in many respects—it is a question unlikely to arise.

397. Would you be good enough to send the secretary of this Committee a copy of that document?—Certainly.*

398. You have heard the evidence given just now by Mr Atkinson as to the circumstances, so far as he knew them, under which these articles were offered for sale to the British Museum. Have you anything to add to what he said, or is there anything in his evidence you would wish to rectify?—As I was not appointed at the time, all I can state is that I know of my own knowledge, is that these objects were not offered for sale in Ireland. There were rumours that certain objects had been found. As an antiquary, I, of course, was interested in all such matters, and I know that no particulars were furnished in Ireland, and that the first particulars we had of the approximate locality or the exact nature of the objects were in the description by Mr Arthur Evans, in his paper read before the Society of Antiquaries.

399. When you read that, did you form any opinion as to whether they were treasure trove, or not?—Certainly. I formed the opinion that they were treasure trove, and I formed a further opinion, namely, that the place of the finding had been concealed; because the paper of Mr Evans describes the fact that the finder had been interviewed, and, notwithstanding that, the name of the place is not given. The articles are stated to have been found "on the north-west coast of Ireland." As a matter of fact I do not know that the locality can be exactly so described, it being on the south coast of Lough Foyle; but, waiving that, it was a general description, "the north-west coast of Ireland," and yet the paper went on to state that the seller, the late owner, had interviewed the farmer upon whose land they were found; so that the actual locality of the find was evidently known.

400. It must have been known, but it was not disclosed on the paper?—Just so; and from the point of view of archaeology that is a blot on the paper, because we cannot ascertain the locality, and, therefore, the precise circumstances of the find: you could not say whether it was in an estuary, in which case it might be a wreck deposit. The whole question of its being a votive deposit turned on the nature of the soil in which it was found. That is a blot on the paper.

401. Have you anything else to say on that head of our reference—the circumstances under which these articles were offered for sale?—I have no direct knowledge, and I could not offer evidence on that point, but I should like to state this. The Director of the museum asked me to attend here to place the matter before the Committee from the Museum point of view. Our position to a museum is that the Government have made certain provisions in Ireland for the collection of objects of antiquity known as treasure trove. These provisions are of a [illegible] definite character. A machinery has been framed for collecting the objects. The Treasury Minute of 10th August, 1860,† sanctioned the employment of the police under an arrangement between the Lord Lieutenant and the Academy, and directed the Lord Lieutenant to issue the necessary notices. In pursuance of that arrangement, notices have been issued, not by the constabulary, but by the Government, and a machinery has been framed in Ireland for the collection of these objects. I produce here the various documents embodying those regulations. First, there is a notice by Sir Thomas A. Larcom, dated 20th March, 1861.

"NOTICE.

"TREASURE TROVE.

"His Excellency the Lord Lieutenant having been informed by the Lords Commissioners of Her Majesty's Treasury that they have been pleased to authorise the payment to finders of ancient coins, gold or silver ornaments, or other relics of antiquity in Ireland, of the value of the articles, on the same being delivered up, notice is hereby given to all persons who shall hereafter find any such articles, that on their delivering them up to the sub-inspector, head or other constable of constabulary in the locality, they will receive, through that department, rewards equal in amount to the full value of the articles.

"THOMAS A. LARCOM.

"Dublin Castle, 20th March, 1861."

This provision does not apply merely to treasure trove, but to all antiquities. What I wish to point out is that there are special provisions in Ireland. We are not under the regulations of treasure trove as applied to England. Owing to the representations made by the Academy to the Lord Lieutenant, a special arrangement was made in Ireland for the employment of the constabulary, and that arrangement included not only treasure trove, but all objects of antiquity. The words are, "Ancient coins, gold or silver ornaments, or other relics of antiquity in Ireland." Then the next document is the instructions issued to the constabulary:—

"TREASURE TROVE.

"1. On the receipt of any articles of treasure trove, ornaments or other articles of antiquity, the officer, head or other constable, to whom the same shall be delivered will give to the bringer a receipt for the same, in the form annexed.

"2. In the case of a head constable or constable, such article, together with a duplicate of the said receipt, is to be forwarded by the constabulary to the officer of the district, who will transmit the same, or any articles that may have been delivered direct to himself, to head-quarters, with all convenient despatch in the manner following:—

"(1) Small articles, or articles of gold and silver (if not of too great weight or bulk), may be sent by post (the parcel being duly registered), or, if no safe and safe opportunity offer, then by hand.

"(2) Articles of bulk may be transmitted by public conveyance (if of value, to be duly registered).

"(3) In the event of articles so transmitted being purchased, the estimated value thereof will be remitted to the officer who forwarded the same, to be paid to the party holding the receipt for such articles. The receipt of payment is to be forwarded to head-quarters.

"(4) In the case of bulky articles, or articles of doubtful antiquity delivered at out-stations, it is desirable that the receipt only for same be sent to the officer of the district, to be forwarded to this office for instructions, before the direction No. (2) in this regard shall be acted on; district officers, in the case of such bulky or doubtful articles being delivered directly to themselves, will also forward the receipt to head-quarters for instructions.

"Although it is desirable that the certificate of finding should be perfected, still this is not to be imperative when the party objects.

"HENRY JOHN BRACKENBURY,
"Inspector-General.

"Constabulary Office, Dublin Castle,
"20th March, 1861."

Then there is a certificate of finding:—

"County of   . I hereby certify that the article (or articles) described at foot hereof was (or were) found by   , of   , in the parish of (describe the place, and if found in the presence of any other)   in the Barony of   , in the county of   , on the   day of   , 18   , in   , on the property of   , being situate in the townland of   , in the parish of   Barony of   , and county of   ." That, of course, is filled up as it best can be in each case.

402. Filled up by whom?—Under the direction of the constabulary.

403. (Sir T. Esmonde.) It has to be witnessed, I think?—Yes.

404. (Chairman.) By whom is given the information?—Yes. Then there is a form of valuation which is not here in force inasmuch as the Academy now pay the finder direct instead of through the constabulary.

Lastly, there is a receipt form to be given by the constabulary to the finder:—

"County of   . District of   . Sub-district of   . Received from   of   , in the parish of   (name companions) the articles described at foot hereof, which I promise to return to the said   , or give him the estimated value thereof, as shall be ascertained and declared under the conditions annexed to this receipt."

The conditions endorsed on the back of the receipt are:—

"1. The value of the article (or articles) to be ascertained by such competent person or persons as shall be named for such purpose by the chief or under secretary), the

* See Appendix IV. † See Appendix V.

Mr. G. Coffey. [illegible]

tender or bringing of same agreeing to be bound by the decision of such person or persons.

"8. If the article or articles be not accepted, it or they will be returned, free of expense, to the bringer."

In practice, the "competent person" has been the Council of the Royal Irish Academy, and the way they act is this. The objects are referred to me, and I am asked to report upon them, and I estimate their value—not merely their bullion value, but what I would consider a fair price to give for the articles, having in view that it is desirable to encourage finders of such objects to bring them to the Royal Irish Academy, that they will get a better price from us than by going to some local dealer. What I wish to direct the attention of the Committee to is that a distinct provision has been made in Ireland for the collection of these articles; it is not a general provision, but a precise and definite one. Now our contention, as a museum, is that if objects are taken out of Ireland in defiance of the Government policy, and behind our backs, and offered to another museum supported by State funds, it ought to be the duty of such museum to communicate with us and ask us whether the particular objects have been offered to us, otherwise the intentions of Government are defeated in Ireland, namely, the formation of a national museum. The object in view was to form in Ireland a national museum. The Government recognised the importance of the collections brought together by the Academy, largely out of their private funds. For instance, they bought the Dawson collection for over £1,000, which was raised by subscription among the members of the Academy without any Government aid at all. It was in recognition of the work the Academy had done in forming a national museum that these provisions were made. And it is important to us that these provisions shall be recognised by other museums, because it is impossible to maintain the representative character of our museum if our series are to be gapped by such objects being taken out of the country. Our position is that the collection of Celtic antiquities—"Celtic" is a name that I do not care to use, because it really does not convey any precise meaning; but the collection of antiquities found in Ireland is the most representative collection of such antiquities at present in the world.

405. Are you, in saying that, including in your comparison the collection of such articles in the British Museum?—No.

406. You say that this is about the best collection in the world. Do you mean including the British Museum?—That does not quite convey what I mean, because as a collection of Irish antiquities ours is necessarily the best collection.

407. What you mean is that the collection of Irish antiquities at present under your charge is, in your opinion, not second to the collection of such antiquities to be found at present in the British Museum?—Certainly. I would say that in several departments it is distinctly superior. For instance, in regard to gold, I made a calculation some time ago for another purpose altogether; we have at present over 570 ounces of prehistoric gold antiquities found in the country. Now the entire collection in the [illegible] of prehistoric gold antiquities found in the British Isles (that is excluding Ireland) would not be, I should say, 100 ounces. In that respect we are quite beyond them. In fact, the only museum in competition with us is what Mr. Arthur Evans has called indigenous gold antiquities is at Athens. For instance, in gold crescent objects we have thirty-one; the British Museum has five, and I think of these, four were found in Ireland. If you take out of what have been called the Celtic antiquities in the gold collection at the British Museum, those that have been found in Ireland, the remainder would not be 60 ounces. A large proportion of the collection comes from what is known as the great Clare find; a very considerable portion of the British Museum collection comes from that find, and they have from time to time got gold objects that have been found in Ireland. That is acknowledged, I think, by all archæologists. Mr. Arthur Evans, when he was over in Dublin some years ago, visited the museum, and I had the pleasure of showing him over it. He wrote to the *Times* a letter, which states substantially what I have just said; in fact, I am practically using his words, and I cannot get a better authority than Mr. Arthur Evans. Then there are several other departments in which we also are very distinctly ahead of the British Museum. In the Bronze Age (Sir John Lubbock will understand what I mean) our collection is especially rich. M. Reinach mentions that we in that particular, for some reason, come out stronger than we ought to do; in fact, in his book, which is the most recent authority, he mentions the chief museums in Europe where the evidence for the Celtic argument is to be found. He gives a number of the chief continental museums, and he mentions Dublin, but he does not mention the British Museum. We have a special class of evidence that renders our museum a very special one in that respect, and our contention would be that it is more important in the interests of archæology that the series should be completed where the representative collection is, than that it should be scattered. All modern archæologists recognise the importance of what is called a long series. You cannot come to any conclusion until you have a sufficiently large series to know that it is representative.

408. Then I understand that apart from any question of national sentiment that articles found in Ireland should be kept there, you also hold that, because you have a particularly good collection of these Celtic gold ornaments, you should have the opportunity afforded to you of securing any articles which are found in Ireland which would be appropriate for the purpose of completing as far as possible that collection?—That is my position in regard to the present objects, some of which are unique.

409. Have you finished all you wish to say upon that branch of the subject?—I do not think it is necessary to go into that in further detail, unless the Committee wish it.

410. Would you be in favour of the establishment of rules or regulations of any kind by the museums of Edinburgh and Dublin and the British Museum respectively for the purpose of giving notice mutually to one another? It would, of course, most often happen in London, where certain articles might be found which might be specially appropriate to a museum in Dublin or Edinburgh. Would you be in favour of some arrangement in order to give the museum specially interested an opportunity of obtaining the articles if possible? How would you put it?—I would put it in this way, that I should like to see an understanding between museums rather than hard-and-fast regulations. I think it is desirable in the interests of the museums of the three countries that the series in the different museums should be made as complete—as "type complete," to use Sir John Lubbock's phrase—as possible, and for that purpose I think it is desirable that the museums should have an understanding that in the case of objects of special interest to a particular institution, that institution should have the refusal of them.

411. Do you consider that, perhaps, what I may call an honourable understanding of that kind would be sufficient without rules or regulations to give effect to it?—I think it would. It does exist to a certain extent, and so far as I know the relations between the British Museum and Dublin have been of a very friendly character. I would put it in this way, suppose a collection is offered in the market, and is going to auction; suppose I happened to be deputed to see it, and report upon it, I might meet Mr. Read, and we would have a chat over it as to what things he specially desired, and what things I specially desired, and we would probably come to an understanding that we would not bid against each other for certain particular objects.

412. I was going to ask you what your view is as to the desirability of framing regulations to prevent undue competition. Of course, that is a totally different question from that of giving notice. What do you say about that?—That is the suggestion I have just been throwing out. That would affect the case of a sale. Very often a collection is on the market, and an understanding can be arrived at. With regard to objects that may be offered independently to one or other of the museums, I think if there was that good understanding—of course cases would arise where each museum would consider the particular object ought to be there, or that it was equally well placed there, but still on the whole I think it would work in a give-and-take spirit, and not to the injury of archæology. I would not go so far as to say that all Irish objects should be retained in Ireland; I should like to see other museums have type-series; but I would say that the series in Ireland should be the representative one; and I say that because at present it is the representative one, and I think it ought to be maintained as such. It would be a great pity that that collection should be impaired by being gapped, as I have described. Occasionally we have objects offered to us which are not necessary for us; they fill a gap in our collection.

413. In this particular case the articles may or may not be treasure trove, but assuming, for the sake of argument, that they are not treasure trove, it appears that the

British Museum in this particular instance did proceed to purchase them without giving any notice to the museum of the country in which they were found?—Yes.

414. Then you consider, as I understand, that that was an exception to the general rule of comity which exists as between the authorities in these different museums?—I think it would be better for archæology that such a comity did exist.

415. But do you consider that, notwithstanding there has been this exception to it, yet a rule or regulation is not necessary, but that it is sufficient to proceed on the assumption that such exceptions to the rule would be so few that it was not worth while to make a regulation at all?—The difficulty of a rule is, as going too far and being too hard and fast. If you made a rule that all objects found in each of the respective countries were to be retained there, that would be going too far.

416. (*Sir Herbert Maxwell.*) Such a rule exists in Greece, does it not?—It does.

417. (*Sir T. Esmonde.*) And in Italy too, I think?—It is constantly broken.

418. (*Chairman.*) Your own view, I understand, is that it would be possible for all practical purposes to carry out the object you have in view by the engendered goodwill of these institutions towards one another, and you would not be in favour of framing rules or regulations even by the governing authority of each institution for that purpose?—If they were framed by the governing body of each institution, that I think would be much better than being framed by an outside body. There I should consider the rule more as a direction.

419. Let me put it in this way. Would you be in favour of directions being given by the governing bodies of these several museums to their officers that proper notice should be conveyed by one museum to the other under the circumstances we have been discussing, and also that there should not be undue competition as between these different bodies?—I think I would be in favour of a rule somewhat to that effect, but the difficulty is that objects may be lost. If articles were brought to the British Museum or the Scottish Museum, and they were obliged to refer to Dublin, there might be a chance of the articles being lost altogether.

420. Then would you be in favour of a rule that so far as possible such a notice should be given—some flexible rule of that sort?—I would be in favour of a flexible rule.

421. Am I right or wrong in supposing that your objection to the rule is rather to its being of too hard and fast a description, and that you would be against such a rule being forced on the museums by outside bodies?—I would.

422. But you would be in favour of the governing bodies of these institutions themselves giving directions to carry out these objects as far as possible?—Yes, that is my view—that each museum should try to help the other.

423. I am putting a little more than that. What I am asking is whether you would go to the extent of having a direction given by the governing body of each of these institutions with a view of as far as possible taking care that notice should be given—that, of course, would exclude a case where the object would be lost altogether—and, secondly, that as far as possible competition between these bodies carried to an extreme point should be avoided?—Yes, I think that substantially conveys my opinion.

424. Do you wish to say anything more upon these subjects?—I do not think there is anything further that I can add.

425. Then have you anything to say upon the third head of our reference, "to consider whether any, and if so, what relaxations should be made in the regulations which prevent the British Museum from parting with objects which it has once acquired." We have been informed that there are no regulations, except regulations

Mr. G. Coffey

18 Dec. 1898.

in a certain sense by statute, and you know what the effect of that Statute is?—Yes, I heard your Lordship explain that to Dr. Atkinson.

426. Would you be in favour of any relaxation of that with a view to a perfectly voluntary relinquishment by the British Museum, if the trustees were so minded, of any articles which they had once acquired?—I think I should be in favour of some relaxation of it. One of the difficulties in a museum is to get rid of a number of things. The provision as it at present exists often hampers you greatly. There are objects which you cannot say are duplicates, and you cannot say that they are not in a sense desirable, but often it might be an advantage to place them in another collection.

427. Have you any such regulation in Ireland?—No; we have no power of parting with anything; we have no permanent regulations; we are not allowed to part with anything.

428. That I believe is under the Treasury Minute, not by Act of Parliament?—I think that is so, but I cannot say precisely.

429. Would you be in favour as regards your own institution and, so far as your opinion goes, as regards the British Museum, of some relaxation which would admit of your getting rid of certain articles which you did not care to continue to keep, and also, I presume, in possible cases of a desirable exchange of articles with other corresponding institutions?—I think I would be in favour of it being possible to relax the rule by, say, the consent of the trustees, which I would make a unanimous consent. I would be inclined to give any trustee a right of veto. You can never tell what the prevailing opinion of the time may be, and to prevent trustees or others running away with things it might be desirable to hedge it round.

430. Have you any other suggestion to make as to such a relaxation if it were made?—I do not think I have anything to add. It is a point I have not very much considered.

431. (*Sir John Lubbock.*) If you have not very much considered it, I should not like to press you upon it. You do not express any very strong opinion on the point?—I do not.

432. Of course, rules must always be in one sense hard and fast; whatever the wording of the rule, it must be obeyed. I rather gathered that the general tendency of your evidence was that there should be good feeling between museums rather than that there should be actual rules?—Certainly; that is my general feeling.

433. You think there would be difficulty in actually putting it in black and white?—There is the danger that if you put it in black and white you may remove the good feeling. You may put them at arm's length, and on a subject like that I think it is rather more desirable to have good feeling, because often a curator of a museum can throw things in the way of other museums; then they are able to divide collections, and so on.

434. And I think I am right in saying that there are a great many things offered which the curator of a particular museum does not himself want, but which he knows others do, and if he is in communication with them he has an opportunity of doing them a good turn, which he might not do if the relations were regulated not by good will but by absolute rule?—Certainly. There is one point I should like to refer to if I may. When you were examining Dr. Atkinson I think Sir John Lubbock asked whether there was any case of a prosecution in respect of treasure trove. There is the case of the Queen *v.* Wilkes, in 1863, which is very much on all fours with this. That was a case in which a labourer had found certain objects which he sold as brass for 6*s.* to two men; one of them was named Wilkes, I forget the name of the other. They sold them to a jeweller for £[illegible], and he melted them. They were prosecuted, and fined £[illegible] each, and imprisoned until the fine was paid, the charge being for unlawfully concealing treasure trove.

THIRD DAY.

Palace of Westminster.

Tuesday, 17th January, 1899.

PRESENT :

The Right Hon. The Lord Rathmore, *Chairman.*

The Right Hon. Sir Herbert E. Maxwell, Bart., M.P.

L. J. Hewby, Esq., *Secretary.*

The Right Hon. the Viscount Dillon, called ; and Examined.

Right Hon. Viscount Dillon.

17 Jan. 1899.

435. (*Chairman.*) You are a Trustee of the British Museum ?—I am, *ex officio*, as President of the Society of Antiquaries.

436. Have you had brought under your notice the reference which is made to this Committee ?—Yes, I have heard it discussed.

437. Do you wish to say anything upon the first head of reference, namely, "The circumstances under which certain Celtic ornaments found in Ireland were recently offered for sale to the British Museum" ?—I have been told —of course, I only know from hearsay—that these articles were really within the reach of the Irish authorities, but that the opportunity was not taken advantage of, and after passing through two or three hands they were offered to the British Museum and bought by them. I understand the Irish museum had opportunities of purchasing them, but did not take advantage of those opportunities. At the same time, I am told they made a large purchase of [illegible] and certain other things. I am told that they had an opportunity of purchasing these things and did not do so, and that they actually bought something else at the same time.

438. I understand that you only tell us that from hearsay ?—From what I am told.

439. I will not press you further about that, because we have heard different accounts in some respects from the people who are actually concerned ; but is there anything else you would like to say upon that head of our inquiry ? That is only as to the circumstances under which the ornaments came for purchase to the British Museum ? —I understand that it was remissness on the part of the authorities in Ireland, who might have bought them and did not buy them. A sufficient interval of time elapsed between the first appearance of the ornaments and their acquisition by the British Museum—an interval of, I think, two years.

440. Your view then, I understand, is that the Irish authorities ought during that interval to have become acquainted with the circumstance that the ornaments were about to be sold ?—Yes.

441. I believe that they contend that, as a matter of fact, the articles were never offered to them, and that they had not an opportunity of buying them ; but that is a question of fact, and you can only speak from hearsay ?—Quite so.

442. Then I pass to the second head of the reference made to this Committee : "To consider and suggest regulations for avoiding undue competition between museums supported out of public funds in Scotland and Ireland on the one hand and the British Museum on the other, for the acquisition of objects of antiquarian or historic interest"—that is, the question of undue competition between State-supported institutions ?—I understand that the present arrangement, which is without regulations at all, has hitherto worked very well. I do not think the British Museum and the Irish and Scottish museums ever work in competition with each other, but they might unavoidably through employing different agents find themselves in competition in the sale room. I understand that in another instance in which Scotland was affected, the Scottish authorities were invited to state what they wished to do, but they preferred to carry out the matter in their own way, and not to give any information which might have led to the British Museum acting differently to the way they did. But there is a good understanding between the three museums, and regulations might hamper the action of the museums very much indeed, whereas the general good understanding, with certain modifications, such as the employment of the same agent by all three museums, would prevent our museums bidding against another in a public sale room. I understand that the chief competitors really with the public museums would be the dealers, and if those dealers can be appointed as agents they would be knocked out of the competition. Of course, there is always the competition of foreigners to be dealt with, but if a good understanding exists between the three museums that gives the best chance of the objects remaining in the British Islands. With regard to the question whether the objects should go to London or Edinburgh or Dublin, I think it is generally understood that, considering the population of the country, probably there are as many students of Irish matters in London as there would be in Ireland, and in the same way with Scottish matters. I think nobody can dispute that people who make inquiries into Scottish or Irish antiquities or history would most likely come to London for the other facilities ordinarily afforded by a large centre like London. Without making the rule too strict, and without considering everything, I think London, as the capital of the United Kingdom, is the best home for objects to come to. There are in London many other facilities for students which smaller places like Dublin and Edinburgh could not offer.

443. Then your view is that there should be a good understanding between these different State-aided museums with a view to their not bidding against one another ; but you, holding in principle that the British Museum is more important as a school of study in such matters for students, would say that the British Museum should have the preference when articles come for sale which the British Museum authorities consider are wanted in their collection ?—I think they should have to a certain extent the preference, and that the good understanding between the three museums would prevent any abuse of the custom ; but formal regulations might prove exceedingly hampering at times. If, we will say, an object of Irish interest came into the market at a time when the funds for the purchase of Irish objects were in a very low state, if the British Museum were debarred from bidding for it, the foreigner might step in and the thing be lost altogether.

444. Suppose, for the sake of argument, the Irish Museum is desirous of having a particular object that is offered for sale, and the British Museum is also desirous to have it—setting aside now the question of funds available, or the question of being able to buy, and looking at it as a matter of principle, where an object comes for sale which we will suppose by the fact of its having been found in Ireland, or from any other local association, would constitute it under the words of this head of reference an object "of peculiar interest" to Ireland—in such a case, I understand, you do not agree with the words following in this head of reference : "The museums situated in the country so interested should be afforded an opportunity of purchasing them before they are acquired by any other institution supported out of the public funds." You say there is a difference of principle there ?—Of course that would depend upon the character of the particular museum.

445. Then let me get you back to this point. If it is desirable that the British Museum as being the most central school should be the first considered, then there is no good making regulations to give the other museums a chance of getting articles which come into competition. The regulations would only be of value to secure for those institutions objects which the British Museum did not wish particularly to have. You are President of the Society of Antiquaries and a Trustee of the British Museum, and what you say will be of the greatest interest upon this question, but the point which lies at the bottom of the controversy clearly is, whether the British Museum, as the central institution, or the museums of Dublin and Edinburgh, as those situated in the country with which the objects are connected, should have the preference—whether in case an object comes for sale which is of "peculiar interest" in the way described here to Ireland or Scotland the claim of the British Museum as a central institution should prevail or not. Do I understand you to say that considering its value as a school of study, the claims of the British Museum should prevail?—I think it ought to a great extent, considering the other facilities afforded for study in a large place like London, which cannot be hoped for, at present at all events, in a place like Dublin or Edinburgh.

446. Of course, you are aware that those collections in Dublin or Edinburgh have been acknowledged by the action of the Government as national institutions for those countries?—Yes.

447. And you also know that they have—at least, they consider they have—very valuable collections of national antiquities, which they allege are superior to the corresponding collections in the British Museum?—I have not seen the collection in Edinburgh, but I have had the advantage of seeing the collection in Dublin, and, of course, there is no doubt that the collection, which was formerly the property of the Royal Irish Academy, and perhaps is still, is exceedingly rich in certain points. I think that is a still further reason for giving the Museum of the Metropolis of the Empire a chance of improving its own collections in those respects. The very fact of their collections being so very rich should be another reason for giving the British Museum every facility for improving its weak points.

448. Then you are very positive on this aspect, I understand: that, although the Royal Irish Academy is recognised as the National Museum for Ireland, and has a very excellent collection, whether for the information of the public or the study of students or scholars of antiquarian interest, nevertheless in case an object comes for sale which would be of importance in completing or tending in the direction of completing the collection in London, you would still say that, the British Museum being the central school, and it being desirable that it should have a more perfect collection, it would be better that the article should go to the British Museum if they wished to get it?—I think so.

449. You quite understand that that proposition is fundamentally opposed to the basis of this reference to us?—Yes.

450. That being so, I presume you would not be in favour of doing anything to support the principle of the first head of our inquiry, which is, "For ensuring that in the case of objects, which, from their origin or associations, are of peculiar interest either to Scotland or Ireland, the museum situated in the country so interested should be afforded an opportunity of purchasing them before they are acquired by any other institutions supported by public funds"?—As I said before, I would trust to the good understanding between the three museums to make allowances if they were not hampered by regulations, and I think such a good understanding would ensure that one museum would see that the other two had anything that was particularly desirable for them. But I think the British Museum should have the first call.

451. I quite understand your position, and it is, of course, directly opposed to the idea of that branch of the reference. Then your view is, that any amenity between the British Museum and the Museums of Dublin and Edinburgh should only go to the extent of giving facilities to the museums of Dublin and Edinburgh for the obtaining of those things which the British Museum did not consider necessary for its purpose?—Just so.

452. I need not ask you any further questions upon that, because all the rest follows. Then there is the other branch of the reference to us, which is, "To consider whether any, and if so, what relaxations should be made in the regulations (statutory or otherwise) which prevent the British Museum parting with objects which it has once acquired." We understand that there are no regulations in existence, except the statutes which govern the museum?—Yes, the Acts of Parliament.

Right Hon. Viscount Dillon.

17 Jan. 1[illegible].

453. You know what the stringency of the existing Act is?—Yes.

454. Would you be in favour of any relaxation of that?—I think some very carefully-worded regulation might be made, and particularly with a view to the assistance of those two museums of Edinburgh and Dublin, but I think to the outer world the very fact of the stringency of the rule is a great protection.

455. You would be in favour of some relaxation of the Act of Parliament as regards the exchange, or the cession by the British Museum of articles which the trustees might be willing to part with to one or other of these two institutions, while maintaining, as I understand, the full strictness of the present Act as against all other customers?—Yes.

456. Would you go a little further, and tell me, have you in your mind any restrictions which it would be wise to impose; for instance, that it should be necessary to have the unanimous consent of the trustees, so that the kind of restriction you have in your mind is "Unanimous" is a very large order; I think a two-thirds majority, or something of that sort, would be sufficient; but there should be a really weighty majority of the trustees in favour of any particular decision, and even then it should only extend to these two national museums.*

457. Is there anything else that you would like to say, post upon any of these heads of reference?—I suggested just now the employment of the same agents by the different museums, so that the museums should not work against each other. I think they should employ the same agent for various classes of objects. In that way you would put these agents out of the field of competition, and they would avoid bidding against each other.

458. (Sir H. Maxwell.) Does your opinion, that the British Museum should have the first call on all objects, extend to objects with no historic association?—No. Where there is a clear and defined association connected with any historic event, then I would make a large concession towards the Irish or Scottish Museum. In the case of, say, gold ornaments being found, about which little or nothing is known, I think the British Museum should have the first chance. In the case of anything connected, say, with the Battle of Bannockburn, or in the case of anything connected with some event in Irish history—articles of some clearly-defined interest of that kind—I think the museum of that particular country should have a very strong voice in the matter; but where the connection is so defined, I should trust to the British Museum to behave liberally to the other two, as she would expect them to behave if they got the first notice of a find. Suppose a thing is discovered in Ireland and it is, if I may use the expression, snapped up by the Dublin Museum, then it would belong to the Dublin Museum, and there would be no question of its coming to the British Museum. But where we all started fair, and the three of us knew that an object was in the market which had a clearly-defined connection with the history of one part of the Kingdom, then I think the museum connected with the particular country should have the first voice. Where there is not the clearly-defined connection, then what I may call the Empire Museum—the British Museum—should have the first voice in the matter.

459. The concrete example in my mind, as you will no doubt have supposed, is the case of the Glenlyon brooch, an object which, rightly or wrongly, is associated with Scottish history, and which the Scottish Society of Antiquaries were extremely anxious to possess? I understand that in that case they refused to disclose before the sale what their action was going to be, and when the sale took place, although the Scottish authorities had appeared rather early in the matter of bidding, the struggle was really between the British Museum and a private individual. I think in that case, the British Museum having sustained the fight, were certainly entitled to consideration. They have since met the case by supplying a very wonderful facsimile, which very few people can tell from the original. Taking into consideration, besides the facilities for study, the greater protection, which I suppose we may admit belongs to the objects in the British Museum than is possible in any other place, I think it is

* See also Viscount Dillon's letter on this subject. Appendix VI.

Right Hon. Viscount Dillon.

27 Jan. 1898.

not requisite that that particular object should be in the British Museum. The number of Scotsmen who take an intelligent interest in the object is probably as large in the Metropolis as in their own country. The preservation of the object is the chief one, and that can be best effected in the British Museum. I think there is no doubt that greater facilities for its protection and preservation exist in London than could exist in any other place at present. So far as regards the lessons to be learned from the design and that sort of thing, and the art contained in the object itself, it can be as well studied from a fac simile, such as was supplied, as from the original object itself.

460. Precisely, and that leads me to the point I was about to put to you. Would it not suffice for the purpose of study in the British Museum to have the perfect reproduction—this fac simile—while the national sentiment which has been aroused—I will not say in Ireland, but the sentiment that has been awakened in Scotland owing to the loss of the object, would be gratified by the possession of the object itself around which the sentiment clings?—I do not know whether the brooch had been before the public in Scotland for any short time, and, therefore, was positively a loss to them, or whether it was merely a question of its discovery. I do not think the brooch was taken from Scotland, was it?

461. I think some Englishman took it from Scotland originally?—Well, and we have got the Coronation Stone. That must not go back.

462. Do you attach no importance to the national feeling which gives the people a pride in these objects?—I attach the greatest importance to it, but I look upon the people of England, Scotland, and Ireland as being all members of one nation. It is merely a matter of going to London, which they would do for other reasons. As I said just now, the facilities for studying and comparison and everything else are so much more complete in London than they can be in any other place. I look upon the three peoples as one nation.

463. In short, you are an extreme advocate of centralisation in these matters?—Not entirely. If that brooch had been closely linked with the history of Scotland, if some great event in Scottish history had turned upon the Glenlyon brooch, it would have been a different matter; but I understand its principal interest is as an object of Scottish art, and it is really a small matter altogether; there is no historic interest connected with it, so far as I know. No great event in Scottish history turned upon that brooch that I am aware of.

464. It is very intimately associated with the history of a family, the history of which is inseparable from the national history?—But it is not associated with any particular event in the history of Scotland.

465. You refer to the special facilities which students have in London compared with those available in Edinburgh and Dublin. What do they amount to?—The libraries of Edinburgh and Dublin are certainly not of the same magnitude as the British Museum library.

466. Surely you are aware that in Edinburgh, including the Advocates' Library, the library of the Society of Antiquaries, and the University Library, there is as much valuable as any single mind could undertake?—Perhaps so for the ordinary individual, but I was referring to persons desirous of making some special study. Take the matter, for instance, of privately printed works and that kind of thing. The British Museum must be ahead—it not it would be very wanting indeed, but I fancy it is ahead—of any library in any other part of the empire. In the matter of illuminated manuscripts, for instance, Dublin and Edinburgh may possess very magnificent manuscripts, but they have nothing like the number and perhaps not as rich examples as the British Museum, which can hold its own with any foreign collection.

467. You think that a student of any particular branch of antiquity might find himself at a loss in Edinburgh or Dublin to a greater degree than he would in London?—In a greater degree, I think so. For certain points he might wish to go to Edinburgh or London, but in the course of his inquiry he must come to London for some reasons.

468. If the British Museum possessed a thoroughly comprehensive and representative collection in every section of antiquity, that would satisfy your desire in that respect?—If it did, but that can never be; it will never be.

469. Is it the case that the Glenlyon brooch filled a gap which existed in your collection before that was acquired?—I suppose it filled one of many gaps.

470. It certainly filled a [illegible] system and development o[f] [illegible] Judging from th[e] [illegible] of things of that class th[e] [illegible] should say it filled a gap. [illegible] filled; there always must [illegible]

471. I do not wish to [illegible] has fallen from your lord[ship] [illegible] that the circumstances con[nected] [illegible] repeated by you from hea[rsay] [illegible] that it is your belief tha[t] [illegible] Irish Academy neglected [illegible] hold of that find before [illegible] Irish Academy. I mean [illegible] I suppose there are othe[r] [illegible] Royal Irish Academy wh[o] [illegible] at heart. The objects we[re] [illegible] hands of Mr. Robert Da[y] [illegible]

472. Are you not awar[e] [illegible] to the British Museum?—[illegible]

473. Is he not also a [illegible] demy?—Yes, and he is [illegible] letting them go to Londo[n] [illegible] circumstances on his part, [illegible] very important for the B[ritish Museum] [illegible]

474. You do not cast [illegible] of the Royal Irish Academ[y] [illegible] any reflection on any em[inent] [illegible] nation in the country.

475. I am glad you do [illegible] in evidence the duties upo[n] [illegible] foresight about them, t[he] [illegible] general interests of the co[untry] [illegible]

476. You have spoken [illegible] the three kingdoms. [illegible] —I do not see why it sh[ould] [illegible] agents who have Europea[n] [illegible] if these agents are keep[ing] [illegible] be prevented from wo[rking] [illegible] foreigners.

477. But is not it the [illegible] the Scottish and Irish [illegible] throughout a number of y[ears] [illegible] they are in the habit of [illegible] Scottish Society is as Mr [illegible] and is employed not onl[y] [illegible] kingdom in securing diff[erent] [illegible] rent classes of objects fo[r] [illegible] agents. For instance, for [illegible] and for pictures and th[e] [illegible] Mr. Wardrobes. I wan[t] [illegible] classes of objects. One [illegible] and one person could not [illegible] experience in different cla[sses] [illegible] acquainted with one class [illegible] Museum authorities some [illegible] that he had been continua[lly] [illegible] to give them some reason [illegible] the one hand, or for giving [illegible] is on the other hand. I [illegible] pital so many men to diff[erent] [illegible] work better, I think, for [illegible] they should have one ag[ent] [illegible] museums. There is no [illegible] museums. I think there [illegible] made and the Glenlyon [illegible] anything but the accompli[shment] [illegible] understood the idea is by [illegible] Europe, and that would [illegible] avoiding any chance of co[mpetition] [illegible]

478. (Chairman.) As [illegible] Irish Academy, I did no[t] [illegible] before because you told [illegible] knew of the subject was [illegible] came to you that they co[uld] [illegible] whatever of this find of [illegible] brought to their notice [illegible] ported in a reasonable pa[per] [illegible] so much as they knew of [illegible] in those very words that [illegible] once applied to the auth[orities] [illegible] posed to look after Treasur[e] [illegible] they had no idea that Mr [illegible] in the way he did, a pur[chase] [illegible] Museum, while they were [illegible] avoiding the Crown on Ir[ish] [illegible] objects. That brings us, [illegible]

was very serious dereliction of duty on their part if they had taken the step which they considered to be the legal and proper one for acquiring this find for the Royal Irish Academy?—I did not wish to convey that the Royal Irish Academy was remiss. I was putting it rather as showing that the general antiquarian spirit in Ireland was asleep. This find was in the possession of an Irishman, and I suppose other people knew it besides Mr. Day, who was an Irishman.

479. That being so, he puts himself in communication, or comes in communication with the authorities of the British Museum—whether he was right or wrong in doing that—and the purchase is effected before the representative of Irish opinion on this particular subject, which we may take to be the Royal Irish Academy, could take any effective step. I will put it in another way. Suppose you were a person living in Ireland, and interested in Irish antiquities, would not you rely on the Royal Irish Academy to look after your interests in regard to such a find as that which we are discussing? You would not consider it your duty to hunt up Mr. Day even if you had heard of his being in possession of these articles; you would rely on your representative body, the Royal Irish Academy, would you not?—I am afraid I should go to the person owning them—that would be my feeling if I was an Irishman.

[illegible] That again is going back to Mr. Day?—I should go to the person owning. A great many societies here, and I suppose the Royal Irish Academy has, local secretaries. Anyone who has to do with local secretaries knows the varying amount of energy that they display; some of them are really only local secretaries in name, and it seems to me the best thing would be to go at once to the person who has the thing in his possession.

[illegible] But we are speaking now of this particular find in the North of Ireland, which was rather a peculiar case. The opinion expressed by the Chief Crown Solicitor in Ireland, which was put before us, was that these articles were found under circumstances which in his opinion made them Treasure Trove. According to the relations between the Treasury, representing the Crown in such a matter, and the Royal Irish Academy, if the law had been observed and the proper course had been taken by all persons concerned, what would have happened would have been this. The person who found the thing in Ireland would have gone to the constabulary or the Chief Secretary, or the Lord Lieutenant, and given information. He would have committed an offence if he had not done so. Then the representatives of the Crown in Ireland would have applied to the Royal Irish Academy, and the Royal Irish Academy would have exercised its power of purchasing at a reasonable price, giving the man something more than the intrinsic value, and then would have obtained the articles in question. That, you may take it from me, is what has been presented to us in the evidence as the normal course of affairs in this particular class of cases. Of course, if the articles are not Treasure Trove, that would all fall to the ground, but you will agree under these circumstances that the Royal Irish Academy, at all events, could hardly be blamed for having lost this find for themselves, considering that as soon as they became aware of its existence they went to the proper authority to reclaim it?—I think there is a great risk in proceeding always according to the formal method. If the then owner of the object has any doubt about his receiving so much as he thinks the thing may disappear altogether; it may be melted down, it may be destroyed, or broken or damaged. In a case like that the best way is to get hold of the object itself first.

[illegible] But, as I understand, in the case of Treasure Trove the person in possession of it has no claim to remuneration at all; that is only a kind of solatium which is given to him as the finder, because it never was his property, it was the property of the Crown?—I think that would lead to the destruction of an enormous number of these things, and therefore I think, considering human nature, the best way if you wish to acquire the thing is to get at the thing itself.

[illegible] That would be rather an argument for altering the law and practice on the subject?—Certainly.

[illegible] I am only speaking now of the Royal Irish Academy and those other Irishmen who were not in possession of Mr. Day's secret. I am not saying anything about Mr. Day now. Do you not think, the law and practice being as I have stated it to you, very little blame can be attached to the Royal Irish Academy for the steps they took in this particular case?—I do not wish to attach blame to the Royal Irish Academy, but as I said just now everybody who knew anything about it was remiss. The British Museum got hold of it because they went to the thing itself—they went straight to the object itself; they did not wait for the legal process.

[illegible] The object itself came straight to them as it happened. If it had come to the Royal Irish Academy in the same way they would have assented to getting it. They took the only step they could. Believing it to be Treasure Trove (as, I think, there is no doubt it is) they took the only step they could, which was to get at the only person who had any claim to make any money out of the treasure at all, and he had no legal claim. The person who found it, if he discharged his proper duty, and brought these articles to the authorities representing the Crown, would probably have got through the Royal Irish Academy some solatium in the shape of money, not because these things were his property, but because he had found them and brought them in the proper way?—Probably he had not sufficient confidence in the liberality of the public body or its power to be liberal.

[illegible] I am not at the moment arguing against your theory that the law ought to be changed in that respect; but, the law being as it is, and the Royal Irish Academy being governed by a Treasury Minute in this respect (in exchange for carrying out which they are allowed a grant from Parliament, so that their duty is quite clear)—can you attach any blame to the Royal Irish Academy for pursuing the course which it was directed to take by the law?—I do not attach any blame, but I think if they had been very eager they would have acted differently.

[illegible] Now, the law being as it is, and the practice being as it is, that is to say that if everybody had done their duty this find would have come into the possession of the Royal Irish Academy—cannot you to a certain extent sympathise with the sentiment which has been aroused in Ireland by this peculiar proceeding on the part of those in whose possession this find was for a time, whereby they have been, I will not say defrauded, but whereby their enjoyment of the articles has been defeated—do not you think that they have some ground for feeling annoyed and disappointed that these articles have gone to the British Museum instead of the Royal Irish Academy?—I should think they would regret that they had obeyed the law so much—that they had followed the legal course.

[illegible] Getting that aside, do not you think, frankly, that there is a ground of grievance from the point of view of national sentiment that the Royal Irish Academy, representing the National Museum of Ireland, has been prevented from having the advantage of this find of Treasure Trove?—I suppose that would be so amongst those people who live in Ireland, but I imagine that the majority of those Irishmen who would see these things would be on this side of the water. The larger number of Irish students would see them on this side of the water rather than in Dublin. If we are considering these articles as objects of instruction, I should imagine that a larger number of students would see them here than if they were in Dublin.

[illegible] That is the view you hold, but you can understand the national feeling which has been aroused in Ireland by these articles not being housed in the national museum in Dublin?—I should hardly call it a national feeling, if I may say so. It is the feeling of what must be a limited number, according to the population, of educated people. It is not what I may call a national grievance. I can understand the Royal Irish Academy feeling very sore about it, and Irish students in Ireland, but it is not a national calamity, I think—particularly as, after all, Ireland is part of England. If these things had gone abroad to some foreign country, I could understand its being regarded as a national calamity.

[illegible] You cannot see objects in the British Museum in London while you are studying in Dublin?—But if you are studying in Dublin you will come at some time or other to England for the purpose of studying. I may just illustrate what I mean. I have been studying Irish costume for some time, and I find the best authorities on that subject are to be looked up in London. For certain points, of course, I should have to go to Dublin, but as to practically the bulk of the information it is to be obtained only in London. I merely mention that as an instance. It is a subject I have been studying for some years.

[illegible] Even taking it from your point of view, would not it be as easy for a student who happened to be in London to go to Dublin in order to see a complete collection, and

Right Hon. [illegible] Dillon.

12 Jan. 1899.

Right Hon. Viscount Dillon.

17 Jan. 1898.

what is admitted, I think, to be a more perfect collection of this particular class of antiquities, as for an Irish student to come to London?—That particular find did not belong to that line of art work which is represented with such particular richness in Dublin, because nothing could be ruder than those particular objects, if they have not, some of them, lost their original form altogether by crushing.

492. Have you seen the collection in Dublin lately?—Yes; about a year ago I was at Leinster House. What I suppose is the glory of the museum are those shrines and book-covers, and so on.

493. We have had evidence to the effect that the most complete collection of old gold ornaments of that class is in the museum in Dublin, and a better collection than there is at present in the British Museum of that particular series—advancing from the rudest kind of gold ornaments, through the stage where they were merely fixed together by pressure, without pins or soldering, or anything of that kind. We have been informed that there is a better series in the Dublin museum of those particular gold ornaments, of which the find with which we are now dealing is mainly composed, than there is in the British Museum?—Of course those ornaments are not, the whole of them, necessarily of Irish work.

494. I know that that has been contended. Some of them are, I think, admittedly Irish work?—Yes, the torques, for instance.

495. But be they Irish work or not, is there not in the Dublin museum a very complete series of specimens of that old gold work, supposed to belong to what is called the late Celtic period? Is it not admitted that the Dublin collection is an exceptionally good one, and at least as good, if not better, than the corresponding collection in London?—That may very well be, but if that is the case there are not objects which would fill up any particular gap in the Irish collection.

496. They think it would fill a gap. Now there is one other question I should like to ask you. You say you think there is more complete and more safe custody of such objects as these in the British Museum than there could be in Dublin or Edinburgh. I do not myself know about Edinburgh, but is not the depository of these things in that fine new building of the Science and Art Department in Dublin as good and safe as it is possible for anyone to make it?—I should have thought that the British Museum was stronger still.

497. How stronger—stronger against what?—Against attacks by thieves and fire, and every sort of damage which can be received by a building. I think the British Museum ought to be, if it is not—and I think it is—the strongest.

498. It is, no doubt, much older, but has not this new Science and Art building in Dublin the best contrived and most modern appliances for safety?—Oh, yes; I was speaking in the same way as I should speak of the British Museum as being a safer place than South Kensington. The Leinster House buildings remind one very much of the South Kensington buildings. I cannot imagine anything much stronger than the British Museum.

499. Since you began your examination I have received a letter written by Sir John Lubbock, who is unfortunately unable to attend to-day owing to an attack of illness, which I am sure all his colleagues here very much deplore. Sir John Lubbock, writing to Mr. Morley, who is also unfortunately unable to be with us, requests that the following questions may be put to you. Some part of the ground I think has been already covered, and you, of course, need not repeat anything you have already said. These are his questions:—"Do you agree with the view that all antiquities found in Ireland should be kept in Ireland, all in Scotland in Scotland, and all in England in England respectively?"—That would be reverting to the state of things at the Creation.

500. "As regards the relations between the British Museum, the Royal Irish Academy, and the Edinburgh Museum, do you prefer a system of specific rules or a general understanding?"—A general understanding.

501. Is there anything you wish to add?—No; I think not.

Sir JOHN CHARLES ROBINSON, called; and Examined.

Sir John Charles Robinson.

502. (*Chairman.*) You are a Fellow of the Society of Antiquaries?—Yes.

503. Are you a Trustee of the British Museum?—No; I am not.

504. You are also Her Majesty's Surveyor of Pictures? —Yes.

505. I will begin by asking you the questions which Sir John Lubbock has suggested. These are Sir John Lubbock's questions:—"When you were making purchases in the South Kensington Museum, was there any friction between the two institutions?"—No, never.

506. (*Sir H. Maxwell.*) Those two institutions being the South Kensington Museum and the British Museum? —Yes. I think I remember no such instance. It is now many years since my resignation, but at the time I was in office there there was a constant and continual system of interchange of intelligence and action between myself and the superintendent of the same department at the British Museum, Sir Wollaston Franks.

507. (*Chairman.*) What was your exact office at South Kensington?—I was superintendent of the art collections and, in fact, director of the museum—at that time, and Sir Wollaston Franks had a similar position with regard to the corresponding collections at the British Museum.

508. I now resume Sir John Lubbock's questions:—"If rules for institutions were laid down, and delays and difficulties interposed, would there not be a danger of antiquities being lost to the nation or intercepted by other purchasers, perhaps in other countries, while the museum authorities were corresponding?"—I think certainly there would be great danger. All these things have to be done rapidly and with great decision, otherwise other purchasers come in. It is not possible, I think, to have correspondence backwards and forwards continually taking place between England and Scotland and Ireland. Things might turn up at any moment. I have always had the feeling that the utmost liberty should be allowed to curators and directors of museums for that reason; they never know when things are coming on the tapis, and unless there is a thorough understanding that a man may act on his own responsibility, as far as possible, there is the greatest danger of other people stepping in. Competition is always very great, and the dealers very often find out when things are going to the hammer or coming forward for private sale before the directors do. On the whole it is, I think, quite indispensable that hard and fast rules should not be laid down to tie the hands of directors of museums.

509. Then Sir John Lubbock's next question is:— "What is in your opinion the value of reproductions for exhibition in museums?"—Apart from the sentimental consideration—which, of course, is very important—I think that reproductions are now in most cases nearly as useful as the original things themselves. The processes of reproduction have become so admirable and so complete that in many instances the *facsimiles* are practically indistinguishable from the originals. That is the case, for instance, with the *facsimile* which the Museum has had done of the Glenlyon brooch. Of course, when sentiment comes in that is another thing. I quite understand that every possible allowance should be made for sentiment; but when objects of art are considered as matters of study, I think that the reproductions that are now made are often practically as good as the originals for that purpose.

510. Sir John Lubbock's next question is:—"Is it easy for anyone who has not made a special study of the question to distinguish a well-made copy from the original?" —That is rather a vague question. To detect these things requires education and constant handling, and seeing the original things. I can quite understand a person making some most egregious mistake if he has not knowledge, because these reproductions are made so well now that sometimes, not often, they may deceive most experienced persons.

511. "Of experts to whom it would be important to have access to an original for the purposes of study, would a greater number be able to examine objects in the British Museum or the Royal Irish Academy?"—I think most certainly the British Museum. I might venture to give an illustration with regard to Edinburgh to show the greater convenience of things being in London than in the provinces, or even in Edinburgh or Dublin. Some twenty-five or thirty years ago the Queen allowed a certain picture to go from Hampton Court to Edinburgh. The

picture had some interest certainly in connection with Scottish history, but it had a far more important and wider interest than that. It was one fold of a great triptych painted for James IV. of Scotland, and containing his portrait. It was originally in one of the churches in Edinburgh. Of course it was interesting from the Scottish point of view, but also it was of very considerable interest and importance as a specimen of early Flemish art, being supposed to be the work of Ugo Van der Goes. Since that time I have had continual applications as to that picture. Many Flemish authorities have written to me for information. At present the picture is housed at Holyrood, at the end of the long gallery where the portraits of the kings are shown. Very few people can see it where it is. Where one person sees it in Edinburgh five hundred would see it if it were in London.

612. Then if a person were desirous of having inspection of an object for scientific purposes, would the object be more useful in the British Museum or in the Royal Irish Academy or in the Edinburgh Museum?—I think in the British Museum, certainly.

613. "Do you agree with Mr. Read that as regards the gold ornaments found in the north of Ireland, and which have given rise to the present inquiry, there is no valid reason to conclude they were made in Ireland?"—I cannot answer that because I have not seen them, and that is a matter in which I am not specially interested.

614. "Are you in favour of changing the Act of Parliament under which the Trustees of the British Museum are bound, except in certain specified cases, to keep all objects which have once been incorporated in the national collection?"—Yes, I certainly am. I think it ought to be changed. I quite agree with Lord Dillon that it should be changed to some extent, and I think I would go rather further, perhaps, than he seemed inclined to go in that matter. In fact, I agree with his evidence entirely.

615. That concludes the questions which Sir John Lubbock desired to be put in his absence. Now will you allow me to ask you on behalf of the Committee if you will give us your views, which no doubt will be of great interest to the public, on the particular point you have just alluded to, as to how far you would go in the relaxation of the present Act of Parliament, which, as you know, prevents the British Museum parting with anything that it has once received except in two specific cases, which are, where the object is a duplicate, or where it is for some reason unfit for the collection?—I think I should apply the same or similar rules that pertain now in the case of South Kensington, which would give the Trustees and directors almost full liberty to circulate or transfer objects. I think the two institutions should have the same rules. I do not see why one should be allowed to circulate and transfer objects to provincial museums and the other not. I can see no reason why there should be that difference. The museums are very similar in their nature; they have in most respects the same things in view, and I take it the same law should prevail in both.

616. In the South Kensington Museum and the British Museum?—Yes.

617. You are aware that there is a regulation in existence (I suppose "regulation" is the proper word to use) which has been instituted on this very point. It was handed in to us during the evidence of Sir Edward Maunde Thompson. The regulation is dated in May, 1854. Were you at that time at South Kensington?—Yes.

618. "At Whitehall, 12th May, 1854. By the Right Honourable the Lords of the Committee of Her Majesty's most Honourable Privy Council on Education.

"(1.) The Lord President of the Council reports to the Committee that he has been in communication with the Trustees of the British Museum for the purpose of affording reciprocal benefit to both the Science and Art Department and the British Museum in the purchase of works of Art. The following is the mutual understanding of both [illegible]." Of course a "mutual understanding" which is laid down by the Lord President of the Council is practically a binding law of the museum?—Certainly.

619. "(2) Works of art belonging to classical epochs are to be considered as the especial province of the British Museum, and the Trustees are to have priority of choice of any offered for sale. The Science and Art Department will only collect a limited number of examples of classical art, and those especially which bear on manufactures.

"(3) When classical objects are offered for sale to the Science and Art Department the vendor is to be referred to the secretary of the British Museum, in order that the Trustees may select what they desire to have.

"(4) If the British Museum refuse classical objects on the ground that it does not want them, or is unable to buy them, then the department is at liberty to buy them at prices not exceeding those asked of the British Museum. If refused on the ground of exorbitancy of price, then the department will not buy at all.

"(5) Whenever an officer of one department ascertains that any objects are for sale of the class which is specially purchased by the other department, information is to be given to such other department.

"(6) To prevent the loss of objects by delay, all communications from the department to the British Museum are to be disposed of, and an answer returned as soon as possible." You are aware of that?—Yes. I recollect that circular, and I can give you the circumstances connected with it.

620. Now you have said to that except in a matter of [illegible] there really is no appreciable difference, except to the eyes of a very expert student of such art, between the facsimile which nowadays can be produced of an object of antiquarian interest and the original?—I should say so in many cases. Of course in some instances that would not hold, but in most matters of antiquity such as the Glastonbury bowl, it would, I think, apply. I could, however, imagine cases in which it might not hold, for instance, in the case of a porcelain vase or a fine painted enamel; but in the case of goldsmiths' work, for instance, the process of electro-moulding or electro-casting is so perfect that things can be reproduced to such absolute perfection that you cannot tell the copy from the original.

621. That would apply to this Irish find as well as to the Glastonbury bowl?—Yes. The thing has occurred more than once. I could give you a curious example. There were at South Kensington in my time two very beautiful early Gothic small salvers, with a little statue in the centre. They were bought, I think, in Spain. After some time a reproduction was made of these, and it appears that the attendant put the reproduction in the place of the original and the original was put in another place altogether. I happened to go round years afterwards, and I looked at the thing, and I said: "It is astonishing how well they do these things nowadays." Then I looked at it and found "Elkington" at the bottom of it. They had put the copy in the place of the original, and it was as good as the other. I myself at first did not know the one from the other.

622. Now, let me carry that a little further. Suppose there were established an amenity, if I may use the word, between the British Museum on the one hand and the Museums of Dublin and Edinburgh on the other, embodied we will say in rules—I will not say regulations, because that is rather a hard word, but rules of direction given by the authorities of each of these museums on the same lines as the rules which I have just read out to you which govern the relations between the Science and Art Department at South Kensington and the British Museum; that is to say that notice should be given as early as possible so as to avoid articles passing to a mere outsider; and suppose further that some preference should be given—either, as Lord Dillon thinks, to the British Museum, or, as some other witnesses before us have said, to what they call the national museums of Ireland or Scotland. As I understand from you it would really make very little difference for the purposes of art study whether there were lodged in any one of these museums the original or a very exact copy of such works of art as we are now dealing with, these gold ornaments and the Glastonbury bowl?—The question of sentiment comes in, however, and I think the sentiment of the Empire at large is as important as the sentiment of Scotland or Ireland. Sentiment exists in Australia and every other part of the Empire, as well as in Scotland or Ireland. I take an Imperial view of this Museum. I regard the British Museum as the Central Imperial Museum. I quite understand that there should be some feeling of rivalry among other institutions, but as regards this point there is scarcely an analogy between the matter of these antique collections and these Irish ornaments. Referring to the regulation of 1854, relating to antique collections, I took the view at that time that South Kensington had no business whatever to meddle with antique things at all. It began as a mediæval or rather as an art museum. There was a very strong and perfect collection of Greek and Roman antiquities already at the British Museum, and I thought we need not meddle with those things at all. At that time

Sir John Charles Robinson.

17 Jan. [illegible]

Sir John Charles Robinson.

[illegible] Jan. [illegible]

Mr. Lowe (the late Lord Sherbrooke), who was then Vice-president, took quite a contrary view. He was a chance, and he said "Oh, if we are going to help the people we ought to have a collection here as well." I said, if so we shall always be opposing each other, and great confusion will be caused, and it will be impossible to carry it out. However, I was overruled, and Mr. Lowe's views were decided upon, and that paper that you have just read was really the compromise between the two views.

523. That is a very interesting explanation of that particular paper, which struck me very much at the time we received it. As I understand, your view is that, so far as it is a question of sentiment, the Imperial sentiment, the sentiment of the larger number, as you consider, of the subjects of the Empire, should prevail over the national sentiment of the particular country in which the museum is placed, which might be supposed otherwise to have some special claim to it?—I think so, generally speaking. I think the question of sentiment should be subordinate rather to that of utility in these matters.

524. But on the question of utility you think the excellence of analogues, so many departments of antiquity at all events, is now so great, that for the purpose of study it would be as well for Irish students, say, to have a copy as to have the original?—Quite so.

525. Or it would suit the student in London so far as the purposes of study went as well to have a copy as to have the original?—It would apply in that way as well; the sword would cut both ways, no doubt. But after all, even students themselves are not exempt from sentiment; any student would, of course, have more reverence for an original than for a copy. No doubt it is one of the good things that can be said for provincial establishments—that they want the sentiment as well as the reality. If the country is to pay for the sentiment, well and good; if, however, you do that you must give a great deal more money to museums than you do at present; and, in many ways, it would on the whole, I think, be dangerous to allow sentiment to have more than a limited sway in these matters.

526. Apart from the question of the art student's advantage, would not you agree that the sentiment in the country with which these objects are supposed to be particularly allied would probably be stronger than the general sentiment of the *Cives Romanus*?—I think you would more likely have ten with your very strong sentiment and ten thousand with perhaps a weaker sentiment. I think in that case the sentiment of the majority ought to prevail.

527. Now, you know what the different heads of our inquiry are?—Yes, I have read them.

528. Is there anything else you would like to suggest beyond what has arisen out of your evidence so far?—Perhaps there is one point in the evidence just given by Lord Dillon that I might say a word about, and that is as to the employment of one agent only. I do not think that that would be feasible in every case. I think the greatest liberty must be left in the hands of the keeper or curator or director of the museum, and he must employ those he thinks to be the best people. If you have one person attending every sale, he would be known, and wherever he put in an appearance it would be known that the nation wanted a particular article, and the price would be run up. My plan, and that of Sir Wollaston Franks, very often was to employ different agents, because then the rest of the people did not know that the nation was bidding. In many cases the contrary plan would have the effect of running up an article to twice the price it might otherwise go for. Perhaps, however, I did not quite understand Lord Dillon's point.

529. Of course, anything that you suggest on that subject is of the utmost importance, having regard to your great experience. Have you any plan yourself to suggest as to alternative to what was put forward by Lord Dillon just now?—I think that is the plan which Mr. Read and others adopt at the British Museum. They employ certain people, and properly, who are well known for certain sections. But to tie them down always to employ one man would, I think, be very wrong. I should give them the utmost liberty.

530. (*Sir H. Maxwell.*) You referred to the advantages which would arise if it were undertaken to supply provincial institutions with duplicates?—Duplicates of actual objects; well, I think they might perfectly well have them.

531. I should like to understand what you mean by provincial institutions?—Any museums that there may be in any great town of the kingdom. I do not know that one would call the Dublin and Edinburgh Museums provincial institutions, but I fancy they stand practically on the same level as Manchester and Glasgow and Birmingham, and so on.

532. Do you include the Edinburgh Museum as a provincial institution?—That is a matter of [illegible].

533. It is not a matter of sentiment entirely. They are public institutions, supported by public money?—True.

534. And are they not administered under statute for the nation?—I do not exactly know how that may be. The Science and Art Department extends its operations to other museums besides those of Edinburgh and Dublin, and there arises the very great question, how far the State can go in that way.

535. But you do not mean to obliterate the old national boundaries or to ignore them?—I do not think I do, but I do not care about keeping them up unduly either.

536. And if you did desire to obliterate or ignore them would it be practicable to do so?—I do not think it would.

537. Would the people consent to your doing so?—No, I think it would be out of the question to try, and I think no one would ever try.

538. You will probably agree that a claim made on behalf of Edinburgh or Dublin for an object of historic interest belonging to Scotland or Ireland would be a stronger claim than any that could be made on behalf of Birmingham or Manchester for an object found in Warwickshire or Lancashire?—I am not quite so sure as to that. I quite understand the strength of the sentiment which would prevail in Scotland and Ireland, but I am not quite so sure that as strong a sentiment would not prevail in Warwickshire or Lancashire. These things do occasionally happen. I am a Fellow of the Society of Antiquaries. We have often had things of that kind sent up to the Society, as to which a very strong feeling has been expressed in a particular locality. But if it were provided in the case of the British Museum that any things found in Lancashire or Warwickshire must be sent to Manchester or Birmingham, that would be found quite impossible. And I think there would be just the same class of claim in the case of Manchester or Birmingham as is made in the case of Dublin and Edinburgh. I do not see how you could admit it in the one case if you grant it in the other.

FOURTH DAY.

PALACE OF WESTMINSTER.

Wednesday, 18th *January*, 1899.

PRESENT:

The Right Hon. The Lord [illegible], Chairman.

The Right Hon. Sir HERBERT E. MAXWELL, Bart., M.P.

L. J. HEWBY, Esq., Secretary.

DR. DAVID CHRISTISON, called; and Examined.

539. (*Chairman.*) You are secretary of the Society of Antiquaries of Scotland?—Yes. It is more proper to say that I am one of the secretaries. I have a colleague, Dr Robert Munro, who is equal with me; and I may mention that it is an honorary office in both cases.

540. Will you tell the Committee what measures have been adopted by the Society of Antiquaries of Scotland for securing objects of national interest for the National Museum?—There are three kinds of measures adopted. Firstly, by donation; secondly, by purchase; and thirdly, by the means of the Law of Treasure Trove. As to donations, a general appeal to the Scottish public for the augmentation and enrichment of the National Museum by donation is prefixed to the published catalogue of the museum; and appeals are frequently made with success to possessors of objects of national interest, even to such as are not Fellows of the society. But a large influence is exercised by the society through its [illegible] Fellows located in all parts of the country, who are [illegible] [illegible] to assist the society in obtaining a scientific record of such discoveries of antiquities as may take place from time to time, by preserving them for exhibition, or securing them as donations for the national collection. [illegible]

[illegible]

541. Will you read any extracts from that report as to the regulations, if any, which exist between the Government and the Society of Antiquaries as to the [illegible] or disposition of Treasure Trove when any finds are made?—I do not know that there are any special regulations. I could tell you the practice.

542. Will you tell us what the practice is?—The practice has varied somewhat according to the views taken by the Queen's Remembrancers who have been in office; but, on the whole, the practice is that:- They lay claim to objects which they hear of as being found if they think it prudent and advisable to do so. They do not, by any means, claim all. When they have an object in their possession they send it to the National Museum to be valued, and their practice is to give the finder the value of the object.

543. (*Sir H. Maxwell.*) The intrinsic value?—The [illegible] value, by which they apparently mean the fair market price for the articles. That is how they are to be interpreted.

544. (*Chairman.*) Then, after it has been valued?—We do not know precisely what amount the Crown takes. We inform them what we consider to be the value; but we do not know what the Crown gives the finder.

545. As a matter of fact have many of these articles of Treasure Trove come into your custody in that way?—Yes. There is a list in the report of [illegible], and they continue to come in considerable numbers. They are not perhaps numerous in a single year, but they are generally very valuable. We do not, by any means, take all that are sent to us. For instance, [illegible]. If we have sufficient [illegible] of that description in our collection we return those that are offered to us to the Queen's Remembrancer, and he returns them to the finder, and the finder can make any use he likes of them. That I believe is the practice.

546. I think in Scotland all articles, be they of precious metal or not, which are found apparently hidden away are considered to come under the description of Treasure Trove?—Yes. That is in consequence of there

* For that Report, see Appendix VII.

Dr. D. Christison.

15 Jan. 1897.

being no actual Treasure Trove law in Scotland. There is no statute or special law on the subject; it is merely part of the common law of the country, and the common law of the country is that articles found which cannot be proved to be the property of anybody go to the Crown. I understand that even articles found in a secret drawer in a cabinet should go to the Crown.

547. Now, will you proceed with your statement?—Since 1886 the society has paid out of the annual grant for purchases the expenses incurred by the Queen's Remembrancer in such cases of Treasure Trove as have been presented to the museum, in terms of the Treasury Letter of 17th January, 1886. That is merely to explain that now out of our £200 a year we pay the expenses incurred by the Queen's Remembrancer in purchasing those articles of Treasure Trove from the finders. That is all I have to say with regard to that subject.

Then as to the nature of the understanding with the British Museum and the Edinburgh Museum of Science and Art for avoiding competition. There has been no formal arrangement, but in each case of important articles coming into the market in Edinburgh and London, intimation was made to Sir Augustus Franks and Sir E. Murdoch Smith, the heads of the departments concerned, that the particular objects were desired for the Scottish National Museum, and in each case assurance was received that there would be no opposition.

548. What do you say as to the reason for the breaking down of the previous understanding and practice in the case of the Glenlyon brooch?—No reason can be assigned. The former procedure was followed by the society; but their request to be allowed to acquire the brooch without competition on the part of the British Museum was refused in terms which implied a denial of the claims of the Scottish National Museum to be relieved from such competition in the case of objects distinctly Scottish.

549. Now, will you give us your views as to the expediency of relaxing the rules which prevent the National Museums from parting with objects once in their custody or possession?—The society thinks it highly desirable, with the view of making each of the three National Museums thoroughly representative of its own area, that they should be empowered to transfer objects of exceptional antiquarian or historic interest to the museum of the area to which their exceptional interest specially appertains.

550. I should like you to tell us what is exactly the history of the Glenlyon brooch which makes it specially valuable to the Scottish National Museum?—Perhaps it may be left to Mr. Carfrae to answer that, as he is more familiar with the question.

551. Is the depository in which your antiquities are kept a building which is well protected against fire and other dangers?—Yes. We have a police watchman on the premises all night; on each flat we have buckets filled with water and hose connected with the main as well. When we first came to the building I had it examined by the fire master, and he told us the precautions we ought to take, and they have been followed since.

552. (Sir H. Maxwell.) Perhaps you will tell the chairman what was the origin of the building?—The origin of the building was this. When we handed over our museum to the Government in 1858 it was agreed that they should in all time provide fitting accommodation for it. Very soon our accommodation came to be very far from fit; part of our objects were in a ceiling below the exhibition room, and the articles in the exhibition room were so crowded together that they could not be properly seen at all. We frequently brought before the Treasury this promise that the Government would give us proper accommodation, but we were always answered in an off-putting kind of way. Finally our vice-president (Mr. J. R. Findlay) persuaded, as you may say, the Government with the building. The Government paid for the site and he built the structure, partly to contain our museum and partly to contain a new portrait gallery initiated by himself. The total sum he has spent on that building I believe is above £50,000, and the value of the part which was built for us was upwards of £20,000. That is the value of what he gave; it does not include the site.

553. (Chairman.) I presume that all modern appliances for the protection of such a building from fire and other dangers were adopted at that time?—Yes, as I have already explained.

554. Now, is this Museum of Antiquities a place of resort for students?—Yes, it is open to the public; it is open to anyone who wants to study for any particular purpose or to copy any particular object, and frequent use is made of that. Students come to consult our library also whenever they like. We have a library of between 8,000 and 10,000 volumes, entirely or almost entirely archæological.

555. I understand the presumption of the society you represent is that articles which have some special interest for Scotland should rather be placed in the National Museum at Edinburgh than in the British Museum in London?—Certainly. To me it seems a self-evident proposition that if National Museums have been established in Ireland and Scotland they should be entitled to everything that will fully represent the area with which they are concerned, and in the same way that the British Museum should have a right to all objects necessary to the full representation of the English area. Speaking not from personal but from general knowledge, I should say that in that respect the British Museum is very far behind us both in Scotland and Ireland. The British Museum very poorly represents the English area at the present time.

556. Should you say that the British Museum had as good a collection of Scottish antiquities as you have in Edinburgh?—Oh no, nothing like it.

557. I understand your practice is—at all events as to Treasure Trove, and I suppose it would be the same as to other articles—to accept such additions to your museum as would tend to make your collection more perfect?—Certainly.

558. And you set aside those which are unnecessary?—Yes.

559. I suppose if it were possible to carry out such an arrangement, if there were some means of exchanging articles, you would be prepared, then, to exchange articles which you did not want, say, with the British Museum or the Royal Irish Academy, if it were possible to do so?—We would be quite prepared to exchange English articles for Scottish things with the British Museum, and in the same way to exchange with Ireland.

560. Is there any obligation upon you to preserve for all time in your museum articles which once come there?—Yes, we are not allowed to part with anything. We have to obtain special leave by applying to the Treasury, but that is the only way that we can part with anything.

561. When you say you are not allowed I suppose that is under some direction or minute of the Treasury that controls you in the matter?—Yes.

562. Then would you be in favour of a relaxation of the Act which prevents the British Museum from parting with any object that has once been placed in its custody?—Yes, the same law being applicable to the Scottish and Irish museums.

563. Would you be in favour of any restrictions as to the opinion of a majority or a unanimous opinion being necessary on the part of the trustees of these various institutions in order to allow of an exchange of that kind?—I should think that the opinion of a majority of the trustees would be sufficient. You would have the opinion of the director, who has special charge of the object, and in the case of the British Museum you would also have to have the opinion of Sir Edward Maunde Thompson to guide the trustees. I should think those decisions would probably be unanimous in every case, but I think the majority ought to be sufficient.

564. Then as to another kind of relaxation that has been made to us, would you be in favour of regulations of any kind for avoiding undue competition between the several museums of the three countries?—Yes.

565. Have you any suggestion to make in that direction?—No; it is not a question that our society has considered. Our council is unanimously of opinion that it ought to be so, but they have not considered any steps. I should not like to give any opinion upon that; it would require a good deal of consideration.

566. Then have you anything to say on the subject of "securing that in the case of objects which from their origin or associations are of peculiar interest either to Scotland or Ireland, the museum situated in the country so interested should be afforded an opportunity of purchasing them before they are acquired by any other institution supported out of public funds"? Would you think it desirable, for instance, that when it came to the knowledge of the representatives of any one of these museums that a certain article was obtainable of especial interest or preponderating interest to one of the others, notice should be at once given?—I think so. Suppose information came to

the British Museum of a Scottish object, they should give preference to the Scottish Museum, and in the same way with the others. I think that would be desirable, and I do not think it would be difficult.

567. Do you see much danger, as has been suggested by other witnesses, that the object might be wholly lost to all the museums and go into the hands of private purchasers in consequence of the delay in purchasing?—There might be a certain danger in the case of things being, as they sometimes are, brought surreptitiously to the museums. But, suppose a man brought an article to my curator, and he saw it was English, he would say to him, a man who offered it: "Why, this thing is of much greater value to the British Museum than to us, and if you offer it there you will most likely get a better price"; or he might be empowered to offer to take charge of it and communicate with the British Museum.

568. Do you wish to say anything on the first head of our reference, namely, "The circumstances under which certain Celtic ornaments found in Ireland were recently offered for sale to the British Museum"?—I am not familiar with that.

569. Is there any feeling, strong or otherwise, in Scotland generally, do you think, on this subject of obtaining for the Scottish Museum objects which have a special interest for Scotland?—There is a strong feeling on the part of the archaeologists of Scotland, including a number of influential nobility and gentry in our society; but it is not a subject that has been ventilated in the public press, and therefore it has not come to the knowledge of the nation at large.

570. (*Sir H. Maxwell.*) I suppose you would scarcely go so far as to say that the British Museum should not contain a complete series, or a series as complete as possible, of Scottish and Irish antiquities?—Oh no; but I think their energies should be chiefly devoted to forming a complete collection of the English area. But it is quite possible for them to have a good representation of the other areas. For example, some years ago there was the sale of the [illegible] collection—which fetched something like £700. The articles were all gathered by a private individual, a man of humble rank; but they were all good Scottish prehistoric articles. We bought about £150 worth for the National Museum, but the others were at the disposal of whoever liked to offer for them.

571. Did you communicate with Sir Wollaston Franks on that occasion?—No. I do not believe that we knew at that time that there was any intention on the part of the British Museum to gather Scottish objects. My own supposition was that they took them if the objects came to them; but that they did not take pains to get them. Of course, Sir Wollaston Franks would hardly fail to know about those articles, as it was a matter of such public knowledge. Every director of a museum is on the look out for that kind of thing, and catalogues are printed and distributed to all who are interested in archaeological questions.

572. Then is it not the practice of the National Museum to exchange information or notices of approaching sales?—No, I do not think so.

573. Do you think it desirable that there should be some such correspondence or relations between them?—I should think it was almost unnecessary in the case of sales by public auction. Of course, in the case of single objects offered for sale to one museum but not belonging to its own area, information should be given to the museum to whose area it appropriately belongs; but in those cases that I have been referring to of sales by public auction I think they are always sufficiently well advertised.

574. I will take the case that has been described to us, not in Scotland but in Ireland. Certain gold objects were found in co. Londonderry, and were offered by an Irish collector to the authorities of the British Museum, who purchased them. The suggestion in my last question is that there should have been some system by which the authorities of the British Museum should have intimated to the Irish authorities that those things had been offered?—Yes, that is analogous to what I have already said—that if such a thing were presented to our keeper he should be empowered to intimate it to the British Museum.

575. Have you ever experienced any collision of interests before the incident of the Glenlyon brooch?—Never.

576. Are you aware that the council of the Society of Antiquaries had fixed any limit beyond which they would not go in bidding for that brooch?—They named a limit, but in naming a limit we always leave our agent power if he sees anything specially interesting in the object, or for any other reason that may seem good to him, to go to some extent beyond the limit. We do not put, in fact, any final limit.

577. Had you to go to the Treasury for funds for this brooch?—We have a right to go to the Treasury for a special grant for an object of that kind, and if we had had sufficient time and warning we should have done so, but the period was too short from the time it came to our knowledge that the thing was to be sold. It is a very long process to get a grant. We have first of all ourselves to meet, then we have to apply to the Board of Trustees. They only meet once a month, so that there may be considerable delay, and then, if they see fit, they forward the application to the Scottish Office, and the Scottish Office sends it to the Treasury, and then it comes back again by the same routine, so that a very long time is occupied. Therefore, when an object comes on the market for only a few days or even weeks, it is hardly possible to get a grant in that time, and we were not able to do it in this instance.

578. Do you recollect what length of notice it was that you got?—Only a few days.

Mr. Robert Carfrae, called; and Examined.

579. (*Chairman.*) You are a member of the Council of the Society of Antiquaries of Scotland?—Yes.

580. And of the Purchase Committee?—Yes.

581. I believe you have been one of the Curators of the National Museum of Antiquities since 1886?—Yes.

582. In discharging those duties you have been in the habit of attending public sales in Edinburgh, and occasionally in London, for the purpose of effecting purchases authorised by the Purchase Committee of articles selected by them as suitable additions to the National Museum?—Yes.

583. What do you do in the case of such articles?—In the case of ordinary articles that do not come to above a pound or so, the Purchase Committee leave it pretty well to myself and Dr. Anderson to arrange the price to be given for them.

584. But in the case of objects of exceptional interest the probable price of which cannot be foreseen, what do you do?—A very large discretion is given.

585. You are given a very large discretion in the matter?—Yes; I am given large discretionary powers. I always take Dr. Anderson along with me if possible.

586. Had you been in the habit of expressing the desire of your committee to acquire particular objects to anyone else?—Always to Professor Archer, who was the Purchase Director of the Science and Art Museum in Edinburgh, and to Sir Robert Murdoch Smith, the present Purchase Director, and also, when I came to London, to Sir Augustus Wollaston Franks.

587. Those were the only departments likely to be competitors with you?—Yes.

588. Had you requested that they would not compete with you in your purchases?—Yes.

589. Was that request on your part conceded?—Always.

590. Now will you tell us exactly what happened in the recent case of the Glenlyon brooch?—In the case of the Glenlyon brooch, when I arrived in London I called on Mr. Read, the successor of the late Sir A. W. Franks, at the British Museum, and informed him that the Purchase Committee desired to acquire the brooch for the National Museum (Edinburgh), as it was an object, the history and interest of which specially pertained to Scotland. To my surprise he took up the position that the British Museum includes Scotland, and refused to give way. He enquired to what price I was prepared to go; but I did not name a limit, because it had been left largely to my own discretion. Opposition from the British Museum, having never occurred before, had not been anticipated in this case, and, consequently, I had no special instructions in view of the contingency, and had no time to write for such instructions.

591. But had any sum at all been named by your committee?—An article of that kind had never been

said, came the Bernal sale, when there was one similar brooch sold. No one had seen this brooch, and it was a matter of speculation as to what it might bring.

592. As a matter of fact, did they or did they not name a figure beyond which you were not to go?—Not a strict figure. None of us had ever seen it—in fact, it was left almost to myself. On the day of sale Mr. Read did not bid, but stood beside the agent who was bidding for the British Museum. I cannot state positively the details of the bidding up to about £150; but after that the bids of £10 each lay between the agent of the British Museum and myself. My last bid being £210, the agent for the British Museum bade £220 and secured the brooch.

593. Why did you stop at £210?—I stopped at £210 thinking I had gone almost as far as the Purchase Committee would have approved in the circumstances, although I knew that the acquisition of an object so exclusively Scottish in character and interest would have largely outweighed considerations of extreme cost.

594. Then your opinion from what you observed at the sale is that if the representative of the British Museum had not bid against you, you would have got that Glenlyon brooch?—Yes. I understood after the sale that the auctioneer had a private commission for £200; but I was prepared to go above that, and did go above that.

595. But according to your evidence there was no effective bidding towards the close except that of yourself and the representative of the British Museum?—No; none certainly after £150. I think there was none after £100 even, but certainly not after £150.

596. Can you tell us what are the characteristics which give this Glenlyon brooch an especial interest for Scotland?—It is one of three that we know for certain—and there is a fourth that was lost—made at about the end of the sixteenth century. One was already in the British Museum; the Glenlyon is also there now; and the third, the Lorne brooch, is in private hands.

597. Then do you say the British Museum have two specimens exactly the same?—Not exactly, but the same in character.

598. And you have none in your Scottish Museum?—We have none in the Edinburgh Museum. The Lorne brooch is in private hands.

599. Would this Glenlyon brooch be an important specimen for the purposes of your museum in Scotland?—Certainly it would; and under the circumstances we were willing to accept the offer of a replica made by the authorities of the British Museum.

600. Suppose it is a question whether the country where the article was made, or the country whose people desired to have it in their museum, although it was not made in that country, should have the original and the other the copy, which country do you think should hold the original?—The country that made the brooch.

601. Do you know anything as regards the Irish case that we have been investigating. Have you any particular knowledge on that subject, or do you desire to say anything about it?—Nothing, except that at that time when I called about the Glenlyon brooch Mr. Read very kindly showed me the Irish articles. I would hold the same ground there; that what has been found in Ireland and has been made in Ireland ought certainly to belong to Ireland.

602. Would you be in favour of relaxing the Act of Parliament as far as regards the British Museum, and the Treasury regulations with regard to your own museum, which require these museums to preserve for all time articles which come into their possession?—Certainly.

603. Would you place any limitation upon the control of the majority of the trustees or the governing body whatever it might be of each of these institutions as to parting with these articles, or would you leave it simply to the opinion of the majority?—The good taste and opinion of the majority.

604. Would you be in favour of regulations being established which would provide that, where it came to the knowledge of one of these institutions that an article was obtainable of special interest to one of the others, notice should be given to the institution so specially interested, before the other institution endeavoured to obtain the article?—I think that should be most carefully done always.

605. And, I presume, from what you have said that you would be in favour of any measures which could be wisely taken to prevent undue competition between State-aided institutions?—Of course.

606. (*Sir H. Maxwell.*) Is anything known of the history of the Glenlyon brooch between the period of its manufacture and the time of its sale to the British Museum?—It has been in the possession of the Campbells of Glenlyon and Troup always, since it was made.

607. It has been associated with a well-known family in Scottish history?—Yes, an old family—the Campbells of Glenlyon and Troup.

608. Have you ever had any difficulty with the authorities of the British Museum before this transaction?—No. I came up here to buy the eleven Lewis chess-men at the Londesborough sale. Sir Wollaston Franks did not oppose me, and I bought them. We have never had any difficulty whatever; quite the reverse. I came up to attend the Bateman sale, at which a number of articles were to be offered from Orkney that we wanted, and Sir Wollaston Franks did not oppose us.

609. Were you acquainted with Mr. Read before this transaction?—I had been acquainted with Sir Wollaston Franks for a very long time, and the last once or twice that I had been in London and called at the museum I saw Mr. Read, but I never had any business transactions till this one.

610. It seems to have arisen from a misunderstanding, does it not?—It arose from the statement that Mr. Read would not give any intimation he considered that the British Museum included Scotland, and that he intended to buy the brooch.

611. He told us that if you had told him the limit to which you were prepared to go he would have then told you his limit?—He should have asked me the limit before he told me that the brooch was to be bought by him.

612. Your recollection is that he told you the brooch was to be bought by him first?—Yes, most distinctly.

Colonel G. T. Plunkett, called in and Examined.

613. (*Chairman.*) You are director of the Science and Art Museum in Dublin?—Yes.

614. Do you wish to tell the Committee anything as to the circumstances under which this find of gold ornaments in co. Londonderry came to be purchased by the British Museum?—I should like to mention that the fact of the gold ornaments being found was carefully concealed in Dublin. I heard of it accidentally, and tried to see the articles, but the silversmith in Dublin who had them in his possession said he was not allowed to show them to anybody, and could not do so without the special permission of the collector, Mr. Day, who was—I was going to say, the owner; but I suppose the Crown was the owner—who was the reputed owner.

615. Then having failed to obtain information in that way, are you aware what steps were taken by the representative of the Royal Irish Academy?—I went at once to the Royal Irish Academy, and informed the officials of the Academy what I saw, and I was told that they already had information that these things had been found in the North of Ireland; they said they were aware of the finding, and that they were trying to recover the articles. It is perhaps rather a curious arrangement in Dublin. The Royal Irish Academy is recognised by the Crown as the body whose duty it is to acquire any treasure trove that is found in the country. With that I have nothing to do whatever, but when they have acquired treasure trove, or when they have bought interesting objects of antiquity which are not treasure trove, then they send them on to me to be deposited in the collections in the National Museum of Science and Art. Then I, as representing the Government in my department, have to exhibit them properly, and provide for their safe custody, but until they come into the museum I have nothing to do with treasure trove whatever.

616. Then I will not ask you any more questions as to the circumstances which preceded the purchase by the British Museum, because you are not officially connected with it?—I really know very little about it except what I have casually heard.

617. Should you be in favour or not of any regulations which would prevent competition between State-aided institutions for articles of antiquarian interest which might be obtainable?—Yes. I think it is very desirable that there should be at all events a clear understanding between those in charge of the museums in London, in Edinburgh, and Dublin, such as would prevent any competition or bidding between them. Probably some very unfortunate—I do not know that a case has ever arisen between Dublin and London; but it is so well, I think, that there should be a clear understanding on the subject, and I think it should be arranged by those in charge of the museums so as not to interrupt the very pleasant relations that at present exist between us and the British Museum; I have constantly received very valuable assistance from Sir Edward Maunde Thompson and Mr. Read. I appeal constantly to Mr. Read for assistance and advice, and information of all sorts on different subjects, and I should like it to be entirely a friendly arrangement. As to this particular find, it is really a matter which concerns I may say lawyers. It is a legal matter. These things are treasure trove, they are the property of the Crown, and, therefore, they ought to be in the hands of the Royal Irish Academy, who represent the Crown for that purpose, and who, as a matter of course, deposit the articles in our museum. But that is an exceptional case. In cases of objects coming into the market I think it would be very desirable that there should be a clear understanding between the various museums to prevent undue competition or bidding against each other, and also as to what articles most appropriately would go to Edinburgh or Dublin than to London. I wish to point out that the museum in Dublin is recognised as and is a national museum, quite as much as the British Museum. It was founded in order to supply the want of a national museum in Ireland, and, in addition to other collections of various kinds in many branches, it was specially intended to hold the great collection of Irish antiquities which had been made by the Royal Irish Academy during the last century, and which they had not space to exhibit. I would point out that these objects, that is to say the present find, and any other objects of the same kind, are of relatively more value to archaeologists and antiquarians in Dublin than they could possibly be in any other city.

618. Why do you say that?—Because we have such a collection of Irish gold and other articles of those early times, from the Bronze Age, through the Later Bronze Age, and the Early Iron Age, and perhaps a little later than that, down to the beginning of our era, such as no other museum has, and no other museum now could possibly make. The British Museum collection of such things is very small indeed compared to ours.

619. Do you consider that this particular find would supply an important link in the chain of your collection in Dublin?—A most important link.

620. What number of persons are there who are interested in matters of archaeological subjects who avail themselves of your exhibitions at Dublin?—We not only have a large number in Ireland, but antiquarians come from all countries in Europe to study the collection of what are called Celtic ornaments in the Dublin Museum. They must come there; they cannot see anything like it at the British Museum. Anybody who wished to study what they call over there the Celtic ornaments, or what are more generally spoken of as Irish ornaments, must go to Dublin to study them. They cannot do so at the British Museum. Therefore, anything which is not an absolute duplication of an object that we have there, is much more valuable if put into the whole in Dublin than if it is put into the much smaller collection in London or Edinburgh, or anywhere else.

621. There is a very valuable library of archaeology, is there not, which did belong to the Royal Irish Society?—The library of the Royal Irish Academy, which is a very short distance from the museum, is very rich in books of archaeology, and the National Library of Ireland is in the same [illegible] with the museum, and there is every facility there for the study of archaeology.

622. And besides that there is the library of the Dublin University?—There is the great library of Trinity College, the University of Dublin, where there are also the very great treasures such as the Book of Kells, and so forth. For any student of Irish antiquities, Dublin is the place he must come to, and to separate any objects which are part of the series from the rest is really a calamity from an antiquarian point of view.

623. I believe the building which is in your charge, in which these antiquities are stored, was built for the purpose not many years ago?—The building was constructed in the year 1885-90 as a museum, and it is as secure from fire and any other accident as any building constructed for a museum can be.

624. I suppose it is probably as guarded against the possibility of fire?—It is specially guarded by the Dublin Metropolitan Police, and Dublin Fire Brigade, and every precaution is taken against accidents of every kind. It may be considered, humanly speaking, absolutely secure.

625. Do you know whether this case of the find at Limavady has created any feeling amongst the people in Dublin who are interested in these matters?—It has created a very strong feeling indeed amongst all who are interested in archaeology and ancient art in Ireland, and beyond that there is a great popular feeling; every newspaper in Dublin, I think without exception, has taken the matter up warmly; but, of course, the feeling is very much stronger amongst scholars and archaeologists, who know the special value of having these things in Dublin.

626. You say you would be in favour of some notice or understanding which would give the museum specially interested in any objects of antiquarian interest which might be obtainable the opportunity of first obtaining them. Are you aware that there is a somewhat analogous set of regulations at present existing between the Science and Art Department at South Kensington and the British Museum for the protection of the British Museum?—I believe I have heard of this before, but I have never seen it.

627. Would you be in favour of something corresponding to those arrangements for the protection of the National Museum in Dublin?—Yes, I should be quite in favour of some similar regulations.

628. Do you think it would be desirable to have any relaxation in the Act of Parliament which governs the British Museum, and in the regulations which I believe oblige the Royal Irish Academy to hold for all time any of these objects of antiquarian interest and other objects which may come into their possession?—I certainly [illegible] think it is very desirable that there should be some reasonable relaxation, so that an object which was of far greater value to another museum than to the museum in which it is, should be passed on by way of exchange, perhaps for articles which would be of greater interest to the receiving museum.

629. Or even, I suppose, if there were no opportunity of exchange, if the governing body of the institution making the concession were willing to part with what they had?—Quite so.

630. Would you govern that by any limitation as to a decision taken by a majority of the trustees, or whatever the governing body might be of these institutions?—As regards objects which are not sent into the museum by the Royal Irish Academy it would, of course, rest entirely with the Department of Science and Art. The Parliamentary chiefs no doubt would only act on the strong recommendation of the director and curator of that particular branch; but in the case of articles which have been deposited by the Royal Irish Academy, another independent body comes in altogether, and it certainly ought not to be done unless the Royal Irish Academy formally expresses the wish that it should be done.

631. That is why I was going to ask you, would you consider it a necessary protection against any temporary freak of a majority that the majority should be an especially large one for that purpose?—I think that is a question for the Royal Irish Academy to answer—as to how they would come to a decision. I think, if the keeper of that particular department, and if the director of the museum agreed to it, and if the Royal Irish Academy officially signified their consent, there would be no danger; but it would be for them to decide in what way they should come to a decision.

632. Is there anything you wish to add to your evidence?—I may say that the floor space which at Dublin is devoted to Irish antiquities is, as shown by a plan which I will put in, more than double that which is devoted at the British Museum to English, Scottish, and Irish antiquities altogether. I also wish to add that it is not only a question of these gold ornaments being placed amongst the series of gold ornaments in the Irish collection, [illegible] that this collection can be studied in Dublin in connection with the barrows, burial places, the inscribed stones, and the antiquities of the country generally, and if they are moved out of Ireland their value as an antiquary is very much decreased indeed.

633. Now I think you wish to add something on behalf of Mr. Coffey?—After Mr. Coffey had given his evidence before this Committee I asked him a few questions, and he said he should like to make a further statement. I asked

Col. G. T. Plunkett

1[illegible] Jan. 18[illegible]

Col. G. T. Plunkett. [illegible]

him to put it in writing, and the following is what he has written to me:—

"To the Director,
"National Museum of Science and Art, Dublin.

"With reference to the article in the Manchester Guardian, December [illegible], [illegible]. My evidence before the Commission on Antiquities regarding a friendly understanding between the museums concerned being preferable to regulations imposed on the museums from without, proceeded on the assumption that the claims of the museums at Edinburgh and Dublin to be the national museums respectively for Scotland and Ireland were admitted; and that it would, therefore, be sufficient to direct the attention of the authorities of the British Museum to the matter to ensure that the prior claims (already, I believed, conceded in principle) of the national museums of Scotland and Ireland to Scotch and Irish antiquities should be recognised in future.

"If a claim is put forward on behalf of the British Museum to be in a fuller sense the national museum not only for England, but for Scotland and Ireland also, as would seem probable from some of the articles referred to, the position is changed, and it will be necessary to examine the validity of such claim."

636. I should like to say that perhaps we might have hesitated to admit this further evidence if that contention had rested solely upon an article in a newspaper, but we have had evidence, since Mr. Coffey was here as a witness, which curiously went the full length of raising that issue, and therefore we shall be very glad to hear what Mr. Coffey has to say.

"Whatever may have been the intention at the time the British Museum was established (a time when the idea of a National Museum, as now understood, can hardly be said to have existed), since the establishment of the National Museums at Edinburgh and Dublin, these museums have not only been recognised by Government as the National Museums for Scotland and Ireland, but are so in fact, by reason of the representative character of their national collections.

"The Museum of the Society of Antiquaries of Scotland was officially recognised as the National Museum for Scotland on its transfer to the Government in [illegible]. Before its transfer to the Government, the Museum of the Society of Antiquaries of Scotland had already attained the leading position in Scottish Antiquities.

"Dr. Daniel Wilson, secretary of the society, in the course of the anniversary address, [illegible], speaking with reference to the transfer of the Society's collections to the Government, which had just been completed, used the following words:—

"'By the establishment of the Society's collections as the basis of a National Museum, I conceive that a responsibility devolves on the Government to place it on a footing worthy of such a position. As the collection of a private society, our museum is one which may be examined with considerable interest, and is even now of much greater extent and value than the Department of Native Antiquities in the British Museum.'

"In the negotiations with Government ([illegible]) for the establishment of a National Museum at Dublin the term National Museum is expressly used, and in the deed of transfer of the museum of the Royal Irish Academy ([illegible]), prepared by Government in pursuance of the arrangements for the establishment of the Dublin Museum, the object of the transfer is described to be to increase the utility of the museum and to ensure its future preservation and enlargement as a national collection.

"But apart from the question of the title of the museum, the collections brought together by the Royal Irish Academy had been recognised for many years previous to its transfer to the new museum as the national collection for Ireland, not only by Government, which had deposited antiquities of national importance in the Academy's museum, but by the common consent of archaeologists, English and Continental. It had been referred to in standard works on archaeology as the 'great Dublin Museum.'

"The importance and representative character of the collections at Edinburgh and Dublin render it impossible for the British Museum to ever hope to compete with them in the departments of Scotch and Irish antiquities, or to occupy the position of a national museum for Scotland or Ireland.

"A few instances will establish this proposition.

"The [illegible] collections of Scotland are at Edinburgh. The finds from barrows and cairns excavated in Scotland are usually exhibited at the meetings of the Society of Antiquaries of Scotland, and are in most cases deposited in the national museum. The special collections from inhabited sites may also be mentioned, and the collections of [illegible] of primitive implements and domestic utensils, etc.

"The British Museum cannot compete in these departments, and can never, therefore, hope to represent the national antiquities of Scotland as a national museum. The collection of stone and bronze antiquities and sepulchral pottery at Edinburgh is also of a more representative character than the British Museum can ever hope to form.

"As regards Ireland the case is equally strong, if not stronger.

"The collection of gold antiquities at Dublin is admittedly one of the first, if not the first, of its kind in Europe.

"The following statement by Mr. A. J. Evans, Keeper of the Ashmolean Museum, Oxford, is sufficient testimony on this point:—

"'What is certain is that the collection of the Royal Irish Academy is richer in indigenous objects of gold work than that of any European museum outside Athens. . . . In their abundance they can only be compared with the treasures unearthed by Dr. Schliemann, but in massiveness these ancient Irish works far surpass the Mycenaean.' (Times, October [illegible], [illegible].)

"The Bronze Age collection is also of great importance, and far surpasses in number and completeness of series the collections from Ireland in the British Museum. The lake dwelling collections of Ireland are also a distinctive feature of the Dublin Museum. The collection of sepulchral pottery may also be mentioned.

"The collection of Irish croziers, shrines, and objects of ecclesiastical metal work is unique. This is a collection which, as regards the croziers and shrines, is final. A second collection of such objects could not be formed.

"These instances are, I think, sufficient to place beyond dispute the fact that, apart from any question of sentiment, it is not possible for the British Museum to occupy the position of a national museum for either Scotland or Ireland.

"Moreover, as centres of scientific activity in connection with the Society of Antiquaries of Scotland and the Royal Irish Academy, and other learned bodies, the museums at Edinburgh and Dublin discharge the functions of national museums in a manner which the British Museum does not, and could not do, for Scotland and Ireland.

"In addition to the above reasons there is the question of space. The British Museum has not space available for the adequate display of national collections. The space given to the Scotch and Irish prehistoric collections respectively in Edinburgh and Dublin exceeds considerably the space allowed in the British Museum to the prehistoric collections of Europe, including England, Scotland, and Ireland. I estimate that the space which will be occupied by the Irish prehistoric collections at Dublin (when the arrangement is completed) will be at least twice that of the entire prehistoric gallery of the British Museum.

"In fact, the idea of a national museum has not been developed at the British Museum in the sense in which the term is applied to the national collections in the museums at, say, Copenhagen, Stockholm, Berlin, and Paris (St. Germain). The museums at Dublin and Edinburgh, on the contrary, have been developed on the lines of the museums mentioned, and fulfil the purpose of national museums for Scotland and Ireland in a higher degree than the British Museum does for England. This is, no doubt, chiefly due to the fact that in England there are many important provincial and local museums in which important sections of the national collections are preserved, as, for instance, the Wiltshire collections at Devizes and Salisbury, whereas in Scotland and Ireland there are few provincial museums, and the collections at the central museums are, therefore, more representative.

"It should be pointed out that the Edinburgh and Dublin museums are not provincial museums, but take rank among the leading museums of Europe in prehistoric antiquities. The Dublin museum has a recognised position on the Continent, and is in communication with the leading Continental museums of a similar class.

"A brief discussion of the importance of the gold antiquities in question to the Dublin collection will illustrate the preceding statements.

"The hollow gold collar with repoussé work decoration is stated by Mr. A. J. Evans to be 'beyond question the most magnificent object of its kind ever discovered.' It is believed to be of native Irish work. The weight of evidence in Mr. Evans's opinion supports that conclusion. The repoussé-work which forms the basis of the ornament of the collar, he points out, is best illustrated by the repoussé-work decorating of a number of objects discovered in the so-called grave of Ollamh Fodhla (Loughcrew, Co. Meath). The nearest approach to the umbrella-like ends of the ornament is found on a shield from the River Witham. The character of the designs and work also recalls examples of the style from Scotland and other parts of England. In Ireland the late repoussé reliefs' of a well-known class of bronze disks 'suggests more than one analogy with those of the gold collar.' Other features recall points in a remarkable bronze ornament in the collection of the Royal Irish Academy (Petrie Collection). But finally, Mr. Evans states his opinion that a certain analogy between the newly-discovered collar and a tubular gold collar in the collection of the Royal Irish Academy, 'some of the decorative scrolls' of which 'distinctly resemble those of the Ulster example,' furnishes 'a distinct presumption that both were made in Ireland,' though the former contrasts with the latter in beauty and boldness of design. Reviewing the whole evidence of the 'find,' Mr. Evans further states in his general conclusions, 'there is at least no question as to the indigenous Celtic character of the most important relic contained in the Ulster hoard. The hollow gold collar, with its bold repoussé designs, is undoubtedly an example of Irish fabric, and it is at the same time the finest example existing of this class of work' (Archaeologia, Vol. 55, pp. [illegible]).

"Shortly before the writing of the paper above referred to Mr. Evans had delivered the Rhind Lectures at Edinburgh, selecting as his subject the Early Iron and Late Celtic Periods, so that he was fresh from a comprehensive survey of the remains of the latter period. His opinion, expressed above, may therefore be considered as final in the present state of our knowledge.

"Of the other objects in the hoard, the gold chains are probably of foreign work. Mr. Evans establishes 'a fair presumption that these objects may have been imported to the British Islands from Alexandria about the beginning of our era.' The alternative supposition, 'that they were of British fabric, closely imitated from Greco-Egyptian models,' Mr. Evans adds, 'at least deserves attention' (page 397). Some points are advanced in favour of this possibility; but the balance of evidence appears to be in favour of the first supposition. In any case, Mr. Evans notes, 'We must admit a very great conformity with various characteristic features of the Late Ptolemaic and Early Egypto-Roman jewels.' The fact that these chains are probably of foreign origin does not detract from their interest in the hoard. On the contrary, it widens the data from which the approximate date of the objects may be inferred. In Mr. Evans's words, 'We obtain, here a chronological landmark of the greatest value.'

"The find as worked out by Mr. Evans is one of the best dated (about the first century B.C.) hoards of such objects which has yet been discovered. This raises it to the position of an important 'historical document.'

"We arrange the gold collection in the National Museum at Dublin in three groups, approximately representing periods.

"(I.) The Bronze Period, in which the gold is [illegible], and soldering (or, more strictly speaking, sweating-on) is known. The central date of this period may be put at about 500 B.C., and it comes down to the Christian era.

"(II.) Thin gold (characteristic of early periods in Europe) ornaments, Late Bronze, or Early Iron Period, no knowledge of soldering, the pieces being held together by being pinched on themselves, or stitched with gold wire.

"(III.) Thin gold ornament—Bronze Age.

"The present objects would form a fourth group in this classification, and are very important in furnishing a datum line for the series.

"The relatively small collections of gold objects in the British Museum from Great Britain and Ireland does not afford material for a representative series such as that in the Dublin Museum (numbering over 400 objects). The hoard of antiquities in question is, therefore, in my opinion of higher archaeological value to the Dublin Museum than to the British Museum.

"I have thought it desirable to write this memorandum in reference to my evidence before the Committee on Antiquities for the reason that, if the principle of separate national museums for Scotland and Ireland is not admitted by the British Museum as governing the relations between the three museums, my views as to the effectiveness of a friendly understanding would be seriously modified.

"(Signed) GEORGE COFFEY.

"[illegible] January, 1899."

[illegible]. Is there anything else you would like to submit to the Committee?—I should like merely to insist on the point I mentioned, namely, that, whatever understanding there should be between the different museums, it should be a friendly understanding between ourselves. I hope we shall continue on the same terms with the British Museum that we have been upon in the past.

CONTENTS OF APPENDICES.

APPENDICES.

APPENDIX I.

Letter from Sir Patrick Coll, Chief Crown Solicitor, respecting the circumstances of the Limavady find

November 23rd, 1898.

Dear Sir,

Referring to your letter of the 18th inst. asking for information as to "the circumstances under which certain Celtic Ornaments found in Ireland were recently offered for sale to the British Museum." About the beginning of February last Dr. Percival Wright, the Secretary of the Royal Irish Academy, called to consult me as Chief Crown Solicitor on the subject, and produced a copy of the "Athenaeum" of 30th January, 1897, which contained a report of a meeting of the Society of Antiquaries of London, at which a paper was read by Mr. Arthur J. Evans (published in "Archaeologia," Second Series, volume 5, page 391) on a certain number of gold ornaments recently acquired by Mr. Robert Day, of Cork, and found by a ploughman who turned them up in ploughing near the sea on the north-west coast of Ireland. Dr. Wright stated that Mr. Milligan, the Secretary of the Royal Society of Antiquaries at Belfast, would give me full information. Mr. Milligan, however, on being interviewed on my behalf by Mr. [illegible], D.I.R.I.C., Belfast, stated he could "give no information."

The Irish Government having written to Mr. Day, who, it was stated, purchased the ornaments, he replied that when he purchased them he was informed that the ploughman who made the discovery sold them to a second party, who, in his turn, sold them to Mr. Wm. Gribben, Jeweller, High Street, Belfast, from whom he (Mr. Day) purchased them in the usual way of trade.

Mr. Gribben, having been applied to, stated that about six months previously a farmer from near Coleraine (he could not recollect his name) came into his shop to have "a gold ornament" weighed, and was referred by him to Mr. Day as a probable purchaser. This farmer stated that one of his labourers had ploughed up the ornament.

This appeared to be obviously [illegible].

The police subsequently made enquiries in the neighbourhood of Limavady and found that about the month of January, 1897, the ornaments were ploughed up by Thomas Nichol, a farm servant of Mr. Joseph Gibson, who lives in that neighbourhood. Mr. Gibson said he gave one to an antiquarian about one month after it was found, but he declined to give the name of the purchaser or how much he got for it. He further stated that he gave 1*l*. each to two ploughmen employed by him.

Mr. Day has, I understand, written to the Secretary of the Royal Irish Academy that he sold the ornaments for 600*l*. to the Trustees of the British Museum.

This, practically, is all the information I can obtain on the subject.

On this information, however, though obviously unsatisfactory, I am of opinion that the articles found were Treasure Trove, and they could now be proved to be so if the persons who know the facts would give truthful evidence.

I refer to the English case of Reg. v. Thomas, 10 Cox's Criminal Law, page 276, which is very similar to the one in question, and also to the Irish case of Reg. v. Toole, 11 Cox, page 75.

Yours truly,
P. Coll.

E. G. Harman, Esq.

APPENDIX II.

Letter from the Scottish Office to the Secretary to the Committee.

Scottish Office,
Whitehall, London, S.W.,
5th December, 1898.

Sir,

With reference to your letter of the 22nd ultimo, I am directed by the Secretary for Scotland to state that a copy of the Treasury Minute, dated the 24th October last, appointing a Committee to enquire into the relations of the British Museum with those of Edinburgh and Dublin, was sent to the Board of Manufactures and to the Society of Antiquaries of Scotland, with a request that they would submit any observations thereon to this Department.

I am accordingly to transmit to you herewith a memorandum dated the 2nd instant from the Society of Antiquaries of Scotland, together with copy of a memorial dated 25th May, 1897, from the Society to the Trustees of the British Museum.

I am to add that a letter has been received from the Board of Manufactures stating that they cordially agree with the views expressed in the Memorandum of the Society of Antiquaries, and do not think it necessary to add anything on their own account.

I am,
Sir,
Your obedient Servant,
Colin Scott Moncrieff.

E. G. Harman, Esq.,
The Treasury.

Letter from the Society of Antiquaries of Scotland to the Scottish Office.

Society of Antiquaries of Scotland,
National Museum of Antiquities,
Queen Street, Edinburgh.
2nd December, 1898.

Sir,

With reference to your letter of the 26th ultimo (S. [illegible]) transmitting copy of a Treasury Minute dated October 24th, appointing a Committee to enquire into the relations between the British Museum and those of Edinburgh and Dublin, and requesting that the Society of Antiquaries of Scotland should submit to the Secretary for Scotland any observations which they wish to place before the Committee, I beg to forward the following observations.

As the first term of reference relates to circumstances in Ireland, of which the Society has no knowledge, it is not in a position to offer any opinion upon it.

In regard to the second term of reference, which relates to the avoiding of undue competition between museums supported out of public funds in Scotland and Ireland on the one hand, and the British Museum on the other, for the acquisition of objects of antiquarian or historic interest, it may be stated that until quite recently no such undue competition as is here referred to had ever taken place between the British Museum and the National Museum of Antiquities under charge of the Society.*

It had formerly been the practice of the Society when desirous of acquiring for the museum any object of special antiquarian interest to Scotland that may have come into the market, to intimate their desire to the British Museum, when the claim of the Scottish Museum was courteously recognised and competition avoided. The same method was followed in relation to the Museum of Science and Art in Edinburgh, and continues to be followed to the present day; but when, on the occasion of the public sale of the Glenlyon brooch—an object of special antiquarian interest to Scotland—intimation was made, in the usual way, to the British Museum by an accredited agent of the Society, he was informed that the

* Perhaps it should be stated for the information of the Committee that by Treasury Minute of 1st July, 1851, the Society is placed in charge of the National Museum of Antiquities under the Board of Manufactures, and that by the terms of their agreement with the Treasury the Society made over to the Nation their entire collections of antiquities, books, manuscripts, coins, &c., with such additions as may hereafter be made to them, so that the Society is precluded from acquiring such objects for itself, and that since 1851 all objects purchased by it for the National Museum have been purchased from public funds.

claim could not be recognised, and accordingly competition took place in the auction room. The superior resources of the British Museum compelled the Society to give way, and the article was lost to Scotland.

In consequence of an action so seriously affecting the prospects of the Scottish Museum, the Society sent a Memorial to the Secretary for Scotland (copy annexed) for transmission to the Trustees of the British Museum, relating the circumstances, and requesting that the article should be transferred, at the price being paid for it, to the Scottish Museum. The Society understand that the substance of that Memorial was communicated by the Scottish Office to the Trustees of the Museum, and they are aware that several noblemen of influence interested in Scottish antiquities supported the application. But the Trustees replied that it was not within their power to alienate any object acquired for the museum. They offered, however, to present a copy of the brooch to the Scottish Museum, an offer which was accepted, under the circumstances, by the Society.

The scientific value and public interest of a National Museum of Antiquities depends entirely upon the completeness of its representative character as regards the country to which it belongs; and in this respect the Scottish Museum, though still deficient in many respects, is recognised as already possessing one of the most representative national collections in Europe. The articles acquired by purchase are almost all Scottish, the exceptions being occasional objects from other countries which it is desirable to have for comparison. The nationally representative character of the Scottish Museum of Antiquities would, however, be greatly impaired were the British Museum to enter into competition with it for Scottish objects; and to prevent this as well as to ensure the attainment of the object of the second reference, it is suggested that, in any regulations that may be adopted for the avoidance in future of such competition, the prior claim of the Scottish National Museum to all antiquarian and historic articles of peculiar interest to Scotland should be fully recognised.

As to the third reference: "Whether any, and if so what, relaxations should be made in the regulations (statutory or otherwise) which prevent the British Museum parting with objects which it has once acquired," the Society consider it highly desirable, with the view of making each of the three National Museums thoroughly representative of its own area, that there should be arrangements to transfer objects of exceptional antiquarian or historic interest to the National Museum of the area to which their exceptional interest specially appertains.

I am, Sir,
Your obedient servant,
(Signed) D. CHRISTISON,
Secretary.

The Under Secretary for Scotland,
Scottish Office, Whitehall.

MEMORIAL referred to in the foregoing letter.

UNTO the Honourable the Trustees of the British Museum, the Memorial of the President and Council of the Society of Antiquaries of Scotland.

SHEWETH:—

That your Memorialists are in the "Charge and Management" of the National Museum of Antiquities (Scotland), and in reference to the provision made for the increase of the National Collections out of Public Funds are under the following directions, viz.:—

Their Lordships will be prepared, within reasonable limits, to consider an application for a contribution from public funds, for, or towards, the purchase of any article of exceptional antiquarian interest connected with Scotland, which may from time to time come into the market.

Negotiations for such purchases should be made after consultation with the Science and Art Department at Edinburgh, so as to prevent the risk of the two Departments competing for the same object.

As regards the purchase of whole collections, or single objects of high value, the Treasury would be prepared to consider any application for the means to buy such collections or single objects when they come on the market.

The foregoing relate to the increase of the National Collection by the purchase of articles of great interest and rarity specially appertaining to Scotland. On the other hand, to effect ordinary small purchases, an annual Parliamentary grant of £200 has been obtained.

Your memorialists, interpreting the direction to consult the Science and Art Department in Edinburgh as a general instruction, have been accustomed to consult the heads of other departments, and have hitherto succeeded in preventing such competition between museums drawing their revenues from public funds.

It is your memorialists' desire to state that for forty years and more it has been their steady aim to make the Scottish collection distinctively national in character, that is, representative of the area of Scotland, and they believe that they have succeeded in bringing the Scottish museum in this respect, though not in size, to occupy a place which is comparable with that occupied by such museums as those of Copenhagen and Saint Germain.

The Glenlyon brooch, an object of very exceptional antiquarian interest, specially appertaining to Scotland, and of peculiar value in the scientific study of its class and period, was offered for sale in a London auction room on the 21st ultimo. The interval between the announcement and completion of the sale being only a few days, your memorialists had not time to apply to the Treasury for a special grant, but they sent one of their number to London with instructions to intimate to the Science and Art Department and the British Museum the intention of your memorialists to purchase this object for the National Museum of Scotland.

The Keeper of British Antiquities and Ethnography in the British Museum however refused to recognise that your memorialists, under the directions of the Treasury which have been referred to, had a prior claim to such an object as this brooch, and declined to withdraw from competition, and the brooch was sold to him for the high price of £[illegible].

In conclusion, your memorialists beg to submit for the consideration of the trustees the question whether, in view of the whole circumstances, it is not just and right that the brooch should be transferred at the price paid for it, to the Scottish Museum, where it would continue to be the property of the nation.

LOTHIAN (President),
D. CHRISTISON (Secretary).

National Museum of Antiquities,
Queen Street, Edinburgh.
25th Nov. 1897.

the expenditure of one hundred pounds a year in the recovery of relics of antiquity, to be carried on upon a plan submitted by His Excellency through the instrumentality of the constabulary of the several counties. And I am directed to transmit for the information of the Academy a copy of the instructions which have been issued for the purpose.

"His Excellency feels assured he may count upon the assistance and co-operation of the Academy in a measure so useful to the public, and calculated to add to the valuable collection already deposited in the Museum of the Academy."

[The printed documents referred to in the above letter were Circular No. 36, headed "Treasure Trove," and signed "H. J. Brownrigg." Notice dated, Dublin Castle, 20th March, 1861, and signed "T. A. Larcom"—also the forms of receipt and certificate of finding.]

5. The Academy willingly agreed to assist to the utmost of its power in carrying out the wishes of His Excellency, and since that time a large number of antiquities, including many torques, rings, and other gold ornaments, have been collected together; the Academy on various occasions having by special private subscriptions supplemented the funds granted by Parliament.

6. When Her Majesty's Government, in 1868, purchased, along with the entire Petrie Collection of Antiquities, the famous "Tara Brooch," the Government of the day was so deeply impressed with the fact that the Academy was the appropriate place of exhibition of these objects that they ordered them to be deposited with the Academy.

7. In like manner, on the acquisition in 1874 of another object, which for beauty of execution takes its place beside the Tara Brooch, viz., the "Ardagh Chalice," it was deposited among the collections of which the Academy is the guardian.

8. Again in 1884, when the Science and Art Department in London purchased, at the Fountaine Sale, the Reliquary of St. Lachtin, the Lords Commissioners of Her Majesty's Treasury sanctioned the transfer of £[illegible] from the Civil Contingencies Fund to the credit of the vote for the Science and Art Department in repayment of the amount expended in the purchase of the object, and deposited the shrine in its natural place with the other historic Irish antiquities.

9. From these facts it is obvious that successive Governments have felt that the Royal Irish Academy is the fitting depository of these monuments of early Irish Art.

10. On the 21st January, 1897, a paper* was read before the Society of Antiquaries of London, by Mr. Arthur J. Evans, on a remarkable hoard of gold objects recently acquired by Mr. Robert Day, of Cork, and in the paper Mr. Evans states that "the objects were found together by a ploughman, who turned them up in ploughing . . . The spot where the treasure was found is near the sea on the north-west coast of Ireland."

Mr. Evans proceeds to describe the various objects in the "find," and coming to the consideration "whether it contained relics of different periods, or that the treasure itself had been collected from more than one source by its original modern possessor," adds:—"With regard to the last possibility, Mr. Robert Day has made most careful investigations, and has completely satisfied himself as to the bona fide character of this find, and that all the objects were brought to light at the same place and at the same time . . . . The fine brown clay with which all the objects were more or less covered also bears out his statement as to their place of discovery."

* Published in Archaeologia, second series, vol. v., p. 391.

11. It is obvious, therefore, from the above particulars that the find is treasure trove, and should have been forwarded by the finder to the Chief Secretary, or to the Academy, or delivered to the Constabulary of the district.

12. The first information which the Council of the Academy had of the matter was the report of the meeting at which the above paper was read, which appeared in the Athenaeum of January 30th, 1897. This report was laid before the Council at its meeting on 1st February, and the matter was referred to the Museum Committee to take such action as was possible with a view to securing the objects for the museum, and with power to communicate with the Crown Solicitor if necessary. The Committee carefully considered the circumstances of the case as published, and both the Secretary of the Academy and the Secretary of Council had interviews with the Chief Crown Solicitor, and brought under his notice the report of the above-mentioned meeting before which the objects were laid.

13. The objects were subsequently purchased by the British Museum.

14. It appears therefore to the Council of the Academy that there has been a distinct breach of the regulations regarding treasure trove found in Ireland, and that it is a matter calling for the strictest investigation, how objects of treasure trove found in Ireland have been acquired by a museum in England without having been submitted to the Chief Secretary directly or to the Royal Irish Academy.

15. The Council feel strongly that, although the British Museum is one of the public museums of the United Kingdom, yet the proper place in which these objects should be deposited is the Royal Irish Academy's Collection in the Museum of Science and Art, Dublin, and that the Treasury should be urged to take steps for the transfer of these objects to the museum in Dublin similar to the steps taken in 1884 for the transfer of the Shrine of St. Lachtin referred to in paragraph 8.

Your Memorialists therefore respectfully request that Your Excellency may be pleased to use your influence with Her Majesty's Government with a view to having these objects, *found in Ireland*, placed along with the other Irish antiquities in the National Collection, deposited in the Science and Art Museum, Dublin, where, but for the evasion of the usual method of dealing with gold objects found in Ireland, they would already have taken their place.

In making this earnest appeal to Your Excellency the Council are not only actuated by their sense of duty with regard to the interests of the National Collection, but also feel strongly that the interests of archaeology will be best served by placing these antiquities in what is admitted to be the most important collection of kindred objects, which it is desirable to render as complete as possible for the purposes of comparative study.

Signed on behalf of the President and Council of the Royal Irish Academy.

✠ W. [illegible], Bishop of [illegible], Vice-President.
Robert Atkinson, Secretary of Council.

Appendix IV.

hereby expressly conditioned and declared that the charge and custody of the said collection of antiquities, coins and medals above transferred shall remain with the said Royal Irish Academy, subject to such regulations and directions as may from time to time be prescribed by the said Lords of the Committee of Council on Education, but so as to leave the Royal Irish Academy as undisturbed in the charge and management of the Museum as circumstances will allow; and also that the funds required to furnish the requisite means for the preservation and exhibition thereof, and to pay the salaries of the present officers of the Museum, who are to become officers of the Science and Art Department, and for the purchase of Irish antiquities as at present voted, under the existing Treasure Trove Regulations, Ireland, are to be provided by an estimate to be submitted to Parliament each year.

In witness whereof the said Royal Irish Academy and the said Lords of the Committee of Council on Education have caused their respective corporate seals to be affixed hereto this 19th day of August, 1890.

Present when the corporate seal of the Royal Irish Academy was affixed:—

SAMUEL HAUGHTON, President.
M. H. CLOSE, Treasurer.

Present when the corporate seal of the Department of Science and Art was affixed:

A. J. R. TRENDELL,
Acting Chief Clerk.
EDWARD BELSHAW,
Clerk of Upper Division.

APPENDIX V.

Appendix V.

TREASURE TROVE.

Return to an Address of the House of Lords, dated 15th July, 18[illegible].

(182) (The Lord Talbot de Malahide.)

"Copy of Treasury Minute, dated 16th August, 1860."

"Write to the Secretary for Ireland in reference to Major-General Larcom's Letter of [figures defective] March respecting treasure trove in Ireland. State that my Lords will be prepared to sanction the expenditure (estimated at about 100l. a year) which may be incurred in carrying out the plan approved of by the Lord Lieutenant for preserving relics of antiquity through the instrumentality of the Constabulary, and that my Lords request that his Excellency will cause the necessary notices and instructions to be given accordingly. Transmit for the information of his Excellency a copy of the Circular and Notice issued in Scotland by the Queen's and Lord Treasurer's Remembrancer.

"Write to Mr. Waddington that my Lords have requested the Lord Lieutenant of Ireland to cause instructions to be prepared and notices given through the Constabulary of that country with a view to the recovery of treasure trove; and, in reference to Mr. Waddington's letter of 12th July (11,738) and Mr. Henderson's letter of 9th May, request that, as Secretary Sir George Lewis sees no objection to the employment of the police in this country for the same purpose, he will take such means as he may consider proper with a view to the same object.

"Transmit also to Mr. Waddington, for the information of Secretary Sir George Lewis, a copy of the circular and notice of Mr. Henderson."

APPENDIX VI.

Appendix VI.

LETTER from VISCOUNT DILLON respecting relaxation of the statutory restrictions which prevent the BRITISH MUSEUM from parting with objects once acquired.

"Ditchley, Enstone,
"10/2/28.

"Dear Lord [illegible],—

"I fear I hardly made it clear when before the Museums Committee, how strongly I feel that it would be quite opposed to the best interests of science, were objects once placed in the British Museum to be removable on grounds other than those already recognised.

"In the very rare instances in which such a removal is necessary, the existing machinery can always be employed, but any greater facility for such action would, I am sure, be prejudicial to the existing collection, and would in some cases deter intending donors from adding to the valuable store.

"I hope you will pardon my thus irregularly addressing you after having had the opportunity of expressing my opinion, but I fear I did so but feebly.

"Yours faithfully,

"DILLON."

APPENDIX VII.

Appendix VII.

REPORT ON THE OPERATION OF THE LAW OF TREASURE TROVE.

(Presented to the Council of the Society of Antiquaries of Scotland by the Secretaries in 18[illegible].)

By instructions from the Committee of Council of the Society of Antiquaries of Scotland, the secretaries have drawn up the following report for the information of the Council, on the operation of the Law of Treasure Trove in securing archaeological "finds" for the National Museum of Antiquities.

The museum, which originally belonged to the society, became national property by agreement between the society and the Board of Manufactures (Scotland) representing the Government, and was placed under the society's management by Treasury Minute of 1st July, 1851.

The claim of the museum to archaeological "finds," therefore, is not that of a mere private society, as is too often supposed, but is public and national, and ought to have the support of all patriotic Scotsmen.

Apart from the intrinsic value of the objects, the instructional value of such "finds" to men of science, to artists, to craftsmen, and to the public in general can scarcely be over-estimated. It is, therefore, contrary to the public interest that they should be destroyed, or excluded from public use by individual appropriation, and in all civilised countries measures have been taken to gather them into the National Museums, so as to preserve them for the use of the public. The systems by which this is effected vary in detail, but they are all founded on the common law principle of the right of the Crown to assume possession of treasure trove or other articles of ownerless property.

The National Museum, as such, has no legal claim to these "finds." They are bestowed entirely at the will of the Crown, but the ordinary practice has been for the Crown, when it has enforced its claim on these objects, to offer them in the first instance to the museum.

The carrying out of the law of treasure trove has been entrusted to the Queen's and Lord Treasurer's Remembrancer for Scotland, through whom all transactions between the Crown and museum take place.

Stated in a general way, it is held in Scotland that treasure trove belongs to the Crown, but we are not aware that the right of the Crown has ever been defined by a decision of the supreme court of law in a disputed case. In England also treasure trove belongs to the Crown, but it is defined as gold or silver which hath been of ancient time hidden, whereof no person can prove any property, while other articles found in the soil are not held to be subject to the claim of the Crown. In Ireland there was no application of the law previous to [illegible], but from that date the Royal Irish Academy have received from the Treasury an annual grant of [illegible] for the purchase of treasure trove for their museum.

Down to the year [illegible] the Crown exercised its claims on treasure trove in Scotland without recompensing the finders, except, in an uncertain way, such finders as were "in circumstances to require" rewards. The result was that very few objects in the precious metals escaped the melting-pot. But in that year the Crown proclaimed, that in future the "actual value" or "intrinsic value" of treasure trove should be given to the finders.

In the absence of any decision by the higher court of law as to the precise meaning of treasure trove, a considerable difference of opinion exists as to the objects which should be included under the term. Some would restrict its scope to articles in the precious metals, while others include "finds" of all kinds. But in practice the Crown authorities have generally adopted a wide interpretation of the term. Appended to this report is a list of the "finds" which from time to time have been claimed by the Crown, and handed over to the National Museum, and it will be seen that it includes every variety of objects of archaeological interest. But it is at the same time true that the administration of the law has failed to secure for the Crown, and through it for the museum and the public, many hoards and portions of hoards, especially of prehistoric gold ornaments of considerable intrinsic value and great archaeological importance, which have either been melted down, or remain in private hands.

Much difference of opinion also exists as to the interpretation of the term "intrinsic value"; but in the Queen's Remembrancer's proclamation of [illegible], "actual value" and "intrinsic value" are used as synonymous terms, and it is the fact that in recompensing finders the Crown authorities have adopted a wide signification, and have awarded a fair market value, which has generally been determined by reference to the Keeper of the museum.

If the facts we have stated are correct, the operation of the law of treasure trove ought to give the museum the first choice of all the archaeological "finds" in Scotland, but this is far from being the case, and that, for the following reasons:—

1. The law has not been carried out on a recognised and systematic plan by the successive holders of the office of Queen's Remembrancer, probably because, in the absence of guidance from legal decisions, they have held different views as to the rights of the Crown, or as to the advisability of enforcing these rights in particular cases.

2. Finders are ignorant as to the state of the law. The finders of treasure trove are usually members of the labouring classes, and are ignorant of the liberal manner in which they would be treated were they to surrender their "finds" to the authorities. Hence concealment of "finds," the breaking up of objects, or their disposal to the best offerer, are still of more or less frequent occurrence. Only once—during the term of office of Mr. Henderson as Queen's Remembrancer—have the rights of finders been publicly proclaimed. This was done by means of a printed circular put up at all the post offices in Scotland, the Procurators-Fiscal at the same time being instructed by circular as to their duties in the matter. Copies of these circulars are annexed to this report (Appendix B.)

3. Landed proprietors are ignorant of the law, or are unwilling to recognise it.

4. There are local objections to the removal of "finds" away from localities to the National Museum.[*]

It is natural that the landowner, when ignorant of the law, should take it for granted that anything found on his estate must belong to him, and even, when informed of the law, that he should have some difficulty in reconciling himself to it. Local objections to the removal of "finds" are also natural, and even even praiseworthy when the desire is to retain them for local museums. Unfortunately, however, not only are "finds" that are deposited in country houses or local museums seldom available for scientific study—owing to remoteness, neglect to label or catalogue the objects, and lack of general care—but, as experience shows, they are liable to be altogether lost, (1) in the case of private collections, through the indifference of owners, who inherit collections in which they take no interest, and (2) in the case of local museums through the actual removal of objects, or the breaking up of the collections. The number of archaeological objects which are first buried in private collections, and either continue to

be thus withdrawn from science, or are ultimately lost sight of, cannot be reckoned; but it must be very great, as there is scarcely a mansion house on any large property which does not contain antiquities picked up in the neighbourhood, and many are known to hold considerable collections. As to the loss to science from the defective organisation of local museums, reference may be made to the reports upon these museums in Vol. [illegible] (new series) of our "Proceedings."

Some of the singular and anomalous results, independently of the loss of objects to the National Museum—which flow, and frequently now, from the want of systematic action on the part of the Crown, may here be pointed out.

1. The finders do not get the recompense to which they are entitled.

2. Landed proprietors and others obtain large sums of money by the sale of antiquarian objects to which they have no legal claim, and which, in fact, belong to the Crown.

3. Our National Museum, although it has no grant[†] from Government for the increase of its collections, is compelled to purchase, often at considerable expense, articles which should, when found, have been claimed as being Crown property.

4. Other national museums, such as the British Museum, employ grants which they receive from Government in the purchase of articles found in Scotland, which are, or ought to have been already, the property of the Crown, and which, were the Crown to enforce its rights systematically, would fall in ordinary course to the Scottish National Museum.

Thus far we have considered the claims of the Crown upon "finds" under the law of treasure trove,[‡] but from the opinions expressed by Lord Kyllachy in the recent case (the Earl of [illegible]'s Trustees) raised by the landowner to interdict the sale by public auction of an urn and jet necklace found at [illegible], it appears probable that the Crown might generally enforce its claim under the common law, as stated in the circular letter issued by the Queen's Remembrancer to Procurators-Fiscal, that "all articles found or discovered, the owners of which are unknown, fall to the Crown." (See Appendix B.)

The memorialists desire to point out, in conclusion, that the prevailing uncertainty of the action of the authorities in not uniformly and rigidly enforcing the rights of the Crown leads to much perplexity and trouble on the part of the Council of the Society in endeavouring to secure for the museum objects which, under a systematic action of the law, would be consigned to their custody as a matter of course. Also that any relaxation in the claiming of "finds" by the Crown must tend to dry up the sources of supply of articles to the museum, a result to which it is to be feared there is an increasing tendency, from the competition produced by the increasing interest in archaeology throughout the country, the spread of local museums, and the increasing market value of objects of archaeological interest.

On the other hand, it must not be forgotten that, were the Crown to enforce its claim in all cases, and to allocate all "finds" to the museum, the unfortunate prejudice against the law of treasure trove, and against the acquisition of objects by the national museum, at present existing among the public and the landowners, might be increased, and the sources of supply to the museum be jeopardised, in another way—viz., by more frequent evasion of the law.

There appears, however, to be a way by which these evils may be avoided without prejudice to the rights of the Crown—viz., by adopting the system in use in Denmark and Sweden, and also in Ireland, of receiving the "finds" and administering the payments to the finders through the museum.[§] One of the principal obstacles to the effective working of the present system is the insuperable dislike of the finders to the Procurators-Fiscal employing the police for the recovery of articles. But the memorialists are strongly of opinion that if the Scottish National Museum were in the same position with regard to treasure trove as the museum of the Royal Irish Academy, by being in receipt of an annual grant from the

---

[*] Since [illegible] it has had a grant of [illegible] a year for five years.

[†] There is no Statute or special Law of Treasure Trove. It merely comes under the common law of Scotland.

[‡] An approximation to this suggestion has lately been made, an arrangement having been come to with the Queen's Remembrancer, whereby the Keeper of the National Museum is empowered to purchase articles of Treasure Trove offered for sale at the Museum.

Appendix VII

Treasury for the purchase of archæological finds, and were to make public proclamation of their position and powers as has been done by the Royal Irish Academy, most of the objects discovered throughout the country would be offered for sale to the museum, while the Crown's claims could still be enforced in cases in which the "finds" were withheld or misappropriated.

In the Appendix, besides the papers already referred to, we have given a brief account of the law of treasure trove in Denmark and Sweden, because it is analogous to our own, and appears to have been carried out firmly and systematically with excellent results (Appendix D).

D. CHRISTISON, M.D., Secretary.
R. MUNRO, M.A., M.D., Secretary.
J. ANDERSON, LL.D., Assistant Secretary.

APPENDIX B (referred to in the foregoing Report).

Appendix B

Copies of Letters of Instruction as to the Administration of the Law of Treasure Trove.

Exchequer Chambers, Edinburgh,
[illegible] November, [illegible].

SIR,—As I have been given to understand that very frequently articles of treasure trove are appropriated by the finders of them to their own use, or retained by those into whose hands they may have come by purchase or otherwise, and not accounted for to Her Majesty, whereby many rare and valuable articles of antiquity are lost, in a measure, to the use of the public generally, being locked up in private museums and collections, instead of being, as is usually the case with reported treasure trove, presented by the Lords Commissioners of Her Majesty's Treasury to public institutions, I beg to call your attention to the fact that, by law, all articles found or discovered, the owners of which are unknown, fall to the Crown, according to the maxim "Quod nullius est, fit domini Regis."

Whenever, therefore, it comes to your knowledge that any such articles have been discovered in your district, I request you to take immediate steps for recovery thereof on behalf of the Crown, and forthwith to report the matter to me.

And I may mention, for the encouragement of the finders or holders of such articles to deliver the same up to the proper officers, for Her Majesty's use, that while the concealment or detention of them is severely punishable by law, the Lords of the Treasury are in the practice of giving rewards to such of the discoverers as are at extra pains to recover them, and of refunding to others the sums they may have advanced in the purchase thereof, when such purchase has been made honestly and not collusively.

While on this subject I would remind you that waifs and strays also belong, and should be accounted for, to Her Majesty, unless the proprietor on whose lands they are found has a grant of waifs, etc.

I request you to make these instructions known to the principal officers in your district.

I am, sir, your obedient servant,
Q. and L. T. R.

To the Procurator-Fiscal of

Exchequer Chambers, Edinburgh,
January, [illegible].

SIR,—With reference to my circular letter of [illegible] November, [illegible], in relation to treasure trove, I beg leave to enclose copy of a notice I have caused to be promulgated, informing the discoverers of all such articles, that they will receive, through this department, rewards equal to amounts to their full intrinsic value, on their delivering them up on behalf of the Crown.

I beg, at the same time, to say that this new arrangement is not intended to disturb the instructions given to the Procurators-Fiscal, in the circular letter above referred to, but that in cases where the articles are not voluntarily given up you are still to take the necessary steps for recovery of the same, on behalf of the Crown, and report the cases to me.

I am, sir, your obedient servant,
Q. and L. T. R.

To the Procurator-Fiscal of

Treasure Trove, &c., appertaining to the Crown.

Queen's and Lord Treasurer's Remembrancer's Office,
Exchequer Chambers, Edinburgh,
[illegible] January, [illegible].

The Lords Commissioners of Her Majesty's Treasury having been pleased to authorise the payment to finders of ancient coins, gold or silver ornaments, or other relics of antiquity in Scotland, of the actual value of the articles, on the same being delivered up for behoof of the Crown, I now give notice to all persons who shall hereafter make discoveries of any such articles, that on their delivering them up, on behalf of the Crown, to the Sheriffs of the respective counties in which the discoveries may take place, they will receive, through this department, rewards equal in amount to the full intrinsic value of the articles.

JOHN HENDERSON, Q. and L. T. R.

APPENDIX D (referred to in the foregoing Report).

Operation of the Law in DENMARK AND SWEDEN.

Appendix D

In Denmark the law assigns to the Crown all treasure or deposits of gold and silver and precious objects, without an owner, found in the earth, and the finder is entitled to receive their intrinsic value on giving them up to the National Museum. "Experience," says Mr Worsaae, "has proved that this arrangement is good in practice, and extremely advantageous to the public collections, especially as it is now widely recognised in Denmark, the finders knowing that they will obtain from the State, whose agents examine and appraise the objects found, not only a more liberal price than from private individuals, but also that any trouble taken to collect and preserve objects is acknowledged by a reward in addition to the value of the metal." The National Museum, besides its ordinary grant, receives funds for the purchase of the deposits, or property of dead men, thus claimed for the Crown.

In Sweden the law and practice are similar, although there [illegible] per cent. is added to the intrinsic value, as an inducement to country people to send their finds to the museum.

INDEX.

[illegible]

www.ingramcontent.com/pod-product-compliance
Lightning Source LLC
Chambersburg PA
CBHW021638270326
41931CB00008B/1076
* 9 7 8 3 7 4 1 1 9 7 2 7 7 *